"That we all need help in our praying is a Christian truism. In this intriguingly titled book, the wisdom of a wise, experienced, and theologically alert pastor-teacher offers help, much help, and nothing but help. Every reader will be grateful for what President Chapell has written."

J. I. Packer, author, professor of theology, Regent College

"Across the years I have learned so much from Bryan Chapell that I thought the laws of mathematics would keep me from learning much more. But it happened again!

"I never close a prayer without saying 'in Jesus' name,' but suddenly I came to see that merely to stack my own agenda for God on top of the word *Jesus* doesn't quite trim the egotism from my conversations with God. Now it is clear: the first word of my prayer should be *Jesus*. This will keep my selfish needs to influence the Almighty in perspective."

Calvin Miller, author, professor, Beeson Divinity School

"Christians are often perplexed and discouraged by the seemingly few answers to prayer they receive. With his usual careful exposition of Scripture and his helpful applications to daily life, Bryan Chapell tackles this issue head-on with a book that should encourage all of us to 'pray and not give up' (Luke 18:1)."

Jerry Bridges, author, speaker, Navigators representative

"This is the book I have been waiting for! Finally, a book on prayer that puts the Person of our Lord before the petitions on our lists. What a novel idea . . . prayer as a means of becoming more preoccupied with the beauty of Jesus' name than paralyzed by the burden of our needs! Bryan has given us an incredibly timely and practical study on prayer. He shows us how the gospel moves us from using prayer as a formula for manipulating God to enjoying prayer as a forum for fellowshipping with our heavenly Father . . . who delights to care for us and bring great glory to his Son, Jesus. If you buy only one book on prayer, I'd recommend this one."

Scotty Smith, senior pastor, Christ Community Church,
Franklin, Tennessee

"This book answers questions about prayer that I have pondered for many years. In view of God's sovereignty, I have wondered how some specific verses should be understood and applied. Bryan Chapell has given me the key."

Nancy Prentis, Bible Study Fellowship teaching leader

PRAYING
BACKWARDS

Other books by Bryan Chapell

Christ-Centered Preaching
Each for the Other
Holiness by Grace
I'll Love You Anyway and Always
The Promises of Grace
Standing Your Ground
Using Illustrations to Preach with Power
The Wonder of It All
1 and 2 Timothy and Titus (with R. Kent Hughes)

PRAYING
BACKWARDS

*Transform Your Prayer Life
by Beginning in Jesus' Name*

Bryan Chapell

BakerBooks
Grand Rapids, Michigan

Published by Baker Books
a division of Baker Publishing Group
P.O. Box 6287, Grand Rapids, MI 49516-6287

Printed in the United States of America

Library of Congress Cataloging-in-Publication Data
Chapell, Bryan.
    Praying backwards : transform your prayer life by beginning in Jesus' name /
Bryan Chapell.
        p.   cm.
    Includes bibliographical references.
    ISBN 10: 0-8010-6527-5 (pbk.)
    ISBN 978-0-8010-6527-9 (pbk.)
    1. Prayer—Christianity. I. Title.
BV210.3.C42 2005
248.3'2—dc22   2005001436

Names of individuals and occasional specifics have been changed in some personal accounts appearing in this book to respect the concerns and wishes of those involved. My debt is great to those who have taught me the gospel of grace by the testimony of their lives.

Published in association with the literary agency of Alive Communications, Inc., 7680 Goddard Street, Suite 200, Colorado Springs, CO 80920.

For a study guide/workbook, please go to www.BryanChapell.com.

To
Lanny Moore Sr.

Valiant leader of God's people
and
humble servant of the Spirit
claiming God as Father
for the
Children of the Covenant
and the
cause of Christ

Contents

Acknowledgments   11
Introduction: *Praying for Change*   13

1. Praying in Jesus' Name: *In Jesus' Name, Amen
   Begin*   17
2. Praying in Jesus' Way: *Not My Will but Yours*   33
3. Praying without Doubting: *Trusting Our Father, the
   King*   49
4. Praying in the Spirit: *Power beyond Our Power*   67
5. Praying Boldly: *As a Child of God*   85
6. Praying Expectantly: *For All Things Always*   105
7. Praying Persistently: *Never, Never Give Up*   121
8. Praying in God's Will: *Within the Fence of
   Righteousness*   141
9. Praying in God's Wisdom: *Within the Fence of
   Prudence*   157
10. Praying Forward: *Paddle and Pray*   175

Conclusion: *In Jesus' Name, Amen*   193
Discussion Questions   195
Notes   203

9

Acknowledgments

I am thankful for the Board of Trustees of Covenant Theological Seminary who provided me a writing sabbatical to complete this book. The constant support and encouragement of this body of faithful leaders has made my years of seminary leadership rewarding and joyful. I am especially thankful for the friendship and wisdom of Chairman Walt Turner, who has been careful to protect my calling and encourage my gifts for the sake of Christ's kingdom.

I am thankful for the Covenant Seminary administrators whose expertise and energies were applied with extra devotion to enable me to have time away from my regular duties. The Lord has greatly blessed me with Wayne Copeland, Mark Dalbey, Donald Guthrie, Brad Hough, and Dave Wicker as colleagues and friends. We are a team!

I am thankful for Mrs. Kathy Woodard. As secretary to the president, she dedicates herself to honoring the Lord by enabling me to do more than I have a right to accomplish, while offering to do more than I have a right to expect.

Introduction

Praying for Change

How would your prayer change if you began where you normally end? We habitually end our prayers with the phrase "In Jesus' name, amen." The *amen* means "truly" or even "I really mean this." But what are we actually saying? We are supposed to be saying that everything we prayed for was offered "in Jesus' name"—for his honor and purposes. When we pray "in Jesus' name," we pray for his sake more than our own. We still present our desires and concerns to God, but we do so in the context of yielding our priorities to Christ's priorities. The final phrase of our prayer reminds us, as well as commits us, to submit all our requests to the glory of Jesus.

Yet that's not always the way we pray. Often we focus on asking God to ease our worries and satisfy our wants before adding "in Jesus' name" as an obligatory spiritual seasoning to make our petitions palatable to God. Some of us may even have been taught to *use* the name of Jesus to "claim the desires of our heart." Such teaching encourages us to end prayer "in the name of Jesus" to get whatever we want. But Jesus is not like a genie in a bottle whom we can command by invoking his name. When we pray, we should be doing more than looking heavenward, believing with all our might that our wish will come true, and instead of repeating, "Star light, star bright, bring the wish I wish tonight," saying, "In Jesus' name, amen."

Two problems immediately arise when we treat prayer like a surefire wishing star. First, we limit God by the wisdom of our wishes. If God were really obligated to do what we think should happen, then God would be tethered to the leash of our understanding. Our wishes would fence God's omniscience within the limits of our brain and restrict his plans to the extent of our insight. But if our wisdom defines the limits of God's, then our world will inevitably unravel. The job we may want for extra income may take us from the family that God knows needs us more. The immediate cure for our sickness may deny doctors an insight that would save millions or may deprive us of the patience that God will use to bring Jesus into the hearts of our children. We must trust God more than our wishes or concede that our world will be controlled by billions of competing wishes that we have neither the power nor the wisdom to control.

The second problem with making prayer a wishing well is forcing the conclusion that prayers, like wishing wells, are fantasies. Though it may seem very holy to say, "I believe that God will be true to his promises and provide what I want," such expressions ultimately deny everyone's faith. Everyone suffers. We live in a fallen world. Biblical prayer does not solve all our earthly problems, and God never promised that it would. Jesus did not even promise his disciples a perpetual bed of roses. Instead, he said, "In this world you will have trouble" (John 16:33).

Prayer does not relieve all suffering, but it assures us that no difficulty comes without a purpose. When we pray "in Jesus' name," we have God's assurance that he will answer our prayer in a way that brings glory to Jesus and furthers his kingdom. When the Lord said of the apostle Paul, "He must suffer for my name," the Savior was not intending to ignore the apostle's prayers but was promising to use them beyond Paul's imagining (Acts 9:16). The difficulties Paul would have been crazy to want, God used to glorify the name of Jesus throughout the world—precisely Paul's deepest prayer whenever he petitioned "in Jesus' name."

The godliest and most prayerful people know from experience the meaning of disappointment, grief, failure, rejection, betrayal, incapacity, and illness. In this fallen world you cannot avoid suffering; you can have peace in the midst of it. You cannot avoid trials; you can have confidence of their purpose. You cannot bind God by your prayers; you can guarantee his blessing. You cannot direct the will of God; you can pray according to his will and rest in the assurance of his love. You can pray knowing that God will marshal the powers of heaven to accomplish on earth all he knows is best for your eternity. Praying in Jesus' name is the key.

Through Jesus we pray without the limitations of our wisdom or faith. We seek the favor of the heavenly Father represented by the Son he loves. We approach the throne of grace without the burden of our sin and with the righteousness of our Savior. We ask for his blessing based on God's wisdom, not ours. We trust in his faithfulness, not in the adequacy of our faith. We petition God with the confidence that earth and eternity will bend to his will on our behalf. All of these assurances are ours as we pray in Jesus' name.

So why wait to the end of a prayer to tag on Jesus' name? Helpful traditions encourage us to add Jesus' name before our "amen" so that we do not forget him. But when our routines have desensitized us to his priorities, then it's time to begin where we end. Praying backwards will inevitably turn our prayer priorities upside down. By saying "in Jesus' name" first, we will more readily discern when our prayers go astray from his purposes, hijacked by our self-interest. Of course, actually saying the words "in Jesus' name" at the beginning of our prayers is not really the point. The message of this book is to put first in our hearts what those words are supposed to mean: "I offer this prayer for Jesus' sake." When Jesus' priorities come first, our prayers will change. They will be less self-oriented, more Christ-directed, more blessed, and ultimately most satisfying to our hearts.

God will honor prayer truly offered in Jesus' name. Such prayer differs from wishes made when we blow out birthday candles. We light those candles to celebrate our years and to fantasize about times made better by wishes fulfilled. By praying in Jesus' name, we petition God to make our life shine for Christ's glory and eternity's purposes. Praying backwards simply ensures that he comes first in our thoughts so that we are prompted to make him first in our priorities. Such Christ-centered prayer is no great sacrifice; for when he is first in our priorities, our needs are first in his heart. The love that flames for us in heaven burns strong and consumes every hindrance to his fulfillment of our eternal blessing. When we pray all for Jesus, he makes our life a candle that lights this present darkness and burns for his glory forever.

1

Praying in Jesus' Name

In Jesus' Name, A~~m~~en Begin

A faithful grandmother was dying of cancer. For many days her family gathered around her hospital bed to encourage her, remember better times, and pray. A friend of mine was a nurse in the hospital. Touched by the tender care of the family, she asked if she could join them in their prayers. Without hesitation they included her.

As the young nurse listened, however, she grew concerned about the content of the prayers. The family called out "in faith" for healing. They told God they had no doubt that he who created the entire universe could re-create health in the body of their loved one. Occasionally a family member would remind God that he had promised in the Bible that if we ask him anything with sufficient faith, we will receive our request. The family called on God to be faithful to his promises by healing the cancer, and they assured my friend, "God will heal."

My friend wondered if it was right to demand that God do what human wisdom determined was best, but the family's prayers were so sincere and bold that it felt wrong to ask questions. Jesus does say in the Bible that if we believe and ask anything in his name, he will answer. Maybe the family was right to pray as they did. My nurse friend wondered how else anyone could pray and still show trust in God's promises.

One day, as my friend finished her nursing rounds, the cancer completed its course. She walked into the hospital room shortly after the suffering woman had died. The family was still in the room, and the young nurse asked if she could pray with them one more time. She was not prepared for the response.

With a steely voice full of new bitterness, the woman's husband replied, "God says to pray and he will answer. We did and he did not. So we're done with that."

Something in us knows that he was wrong, but why wasn't he right to be disappointed in God—or at least disappointed in prayer? If the Bible promises God will answer prayer and he does not, then something must be wrong. Can we trust that God listens and responds to our specific requests, or do we have to spiritualize God's promises into general principles about his eternal providence? Is it right to pray about our daily concerns, or are we imposing on an infinite God when we ask for his intimate care? How does Jesus really want us to pray?

Asking Again—and Again

We should not be surprised that even those with a great deal of spiritual experience need to ask, "Lord, how are we supposed to pray?" After almost three years of walking with Jesus, watching his life, and hearing his words, the apostles came to Jesus and said, "Lord, teach us to pray" (Luke 11:1). You would think they would already know.

Day after day Jesus' disciples had heard his teaching, watched his example, and prayed with him. Early in his ministry, Jesus also took time to teach them to pray to his Father (Matt. 6:9–13). So if even experienced apostles had questions about how they should pray, we do not need to be ashamed that we have some questions too.

Jesus is so patient. He does not condemn or rebuke the apostles for their repeated questions or elementary understanding. Seeing how Jesus reacts to his disciples is important for my own prayer life. When I am tempted to blame myself for not knowing more than I do about prayer, the patience of the Savior calms my heart and draws me to him. I know from his treatment of the apostles that he wants me close and will listen to me even when I need to ask again and again, "Lord, how should I pray?" Of course, I do not usually ask this question in times of smooth sailing. But when life's complexities, difficulties, and surprises storm, I ask lots of questions and am thankful for a Savior who does not grow angry because I must grow in understanding.

Preparing for our rough seas, the Holy Spirit recorded Christ's repeated instructions on prayer in the Bible and also inspired the apostles and prophets to teach us how to pray. The Spirit knows that we will need an occasional review, particularly in rough times. Such patience and concern to help us know how to pray encourage us not to run from our questions but to bring them to our God. He wants us to know how to pray for healing, help, or simple comfort. The concerns of our life are not below his radar screen but are ever before his face. His willingness to teach us again and again to pray tells us how important it is that we come to him again and again.

Praying in His Name—First

When the farmer prays for rain to water wilting crops, and the Sunday school teacher prays for sun to protect the church picnic, whose prayer should be answered? How can we know for certain who is right? Will God simply answer the one whose prayers are best and whose faith is greatest? Surely we have to depend on wisdom greater than our own when we pray. But how do we reconcile this instinctive understanding of the limits of our prayers with the Bible's teaching about praying for whatever we want?

Something in us whispers that it is not right to treat our God like a celestial vending machine into which we place faith nickels to get the jackpot we want. Such faith would seem to put more confidence in our wisdom about how the world should work than in an infinitely wise God. Somehow proper prayer must put more trust in God's will than in human wants; otherwise failure to get the things we want will force us to doubt either the power of prayer or the ability of God.

Jesus taught his disciples not to doubt when they prayed and to expect answers. If this does not mean that prayer is simply a means of snapping our fingers to get God to do our bidding, what does it mean? Answers come when we weigh each word—skipping none of Jesus' instruction to pray with belief and with boldness—and as we simultaneously consider the wisdom of praying backwards.

Praying backwards means we put first priority on the words we say last in our prayers. As strange as it may seem, if we would dare to pray backwards, if we would remember to start where we end (in the desires of our heart, if not in the actual words of our mouth), we would discover the foundation of blessing on which all answered prayer is built. Praying entire prayers in Jesus' name profoundly alters our priorities and powerfully sends our requests to God.

The Privilege of Jesus' Name

Why do we finish our prayers with the refrain "In Jesus' name"? Is this just the religious form of saying, "Yours truly," or "Roger, wilco, over and out"? Is Jesus' name just a "sanctified" period? We know better. The most important reason we pray in Jesus' name is because he says we should:

- "I will do whatever you ask in my name, so that the Son may bring glory to the Father. You may ask me for anything in my name, and I will do it" (John 14:13–14).

- "You did not choose me, but I chose you and appointed you to go and bear fruit—fruit that will last. Then the Father will give you whatever you ask in my name" (15:16).

Though Jesus commands us to pray in his name, the reason we do so is not simply to make sure that we get our prayer formula right. Our prayers are not more powerful because we chant our Savior's name like a magic spell. If we use Jesus' name as some sort of spiritual incantation, then we fall into the error of the sorcerers in the book of Acts who thought that using Jesus' name was just another way of saying "abracadabra" or "shazam" (see Acts 19:13–16). We are not to mimic witches spicing their caldrons with a little eye of newt and tail of squirrel when we add Jesus' name to our prayers.

The Merit of Jesus' Name

Echoing behind Christ's instruction to use his name is the understanding that he makes it possible for us to approach God. When we pray in Jesus' name, we confess that we are not coming to God or asking for his blessing on the basis of our merit. In essence, we are saying, "Lord, there is not enough goodness in my best works to warrant your listening to me or answering my prayer. But, Lord, I am not appealing to you on the basis of my merit. I ask you to listen to me as one who trusts in the blood of Jesus to wash away my sin. By the work of your Holy Spirit, I am united to Jesus, and it is only on the basis of his righteousness that I feel I can approach your holy throne in this prayer."

Praying in Jesus' name is automatically a confession of our unworthiness and a proclamation of his worthiness. By including the name of Jesus in our prayers, we acknowledge:

- He paid the debt for our sins in his suffering and death on the cross. "In him we have redemption through his blood, the forgiveness of sins, in accordance with the riches of God's grace" (Eph. 1:7).
- He provides us union with him so that we are now robed in his righteousness and pronounced by the heavenly Father to be as precious to him as his own Son. "God made him who had no sin to be sin for us, so that in him we might become the righteousness of God" (2 Cor. 5:21).

Thus prayer in Jesus' name is not an incantation to make us worthy of divine attention; it is a confession that we are unworthy of even approaching God apart from the mercy and merits of our Savior. We pray in the name of Jesus to profess our need of him and to proclaim our trust in the provision of righteousness he made for us.

The Appeal of Jesus' Name

We also use the name of Jesus in our prayers to acknowledge what he is doing now. Not only does Christ give us his holy status so that we can approach our holy God, Jesus also intercedes for us. As our resurrected Lord, he now sits at the right hand of the Father to petition him for our good:

- Christ Jesus, who died—more than that, who was raised to life—is at the right hand of God and is also interceding for us (Rom. 8:34).

- Because Jesus lives forever, he has a permanent priesthood. Therefore he is able to save completely those who come to God through him, because he always lives to intercede for them (Heb. 7:24–25).
- My dear children, I write this to you so that you will not sin. But if anybody does sin, we have one who speaks to the Father in our defense—Jesus Christ, the Righteous One (1 John 2:1).

Jesus so loves us that he uses the privileges of his exalted position and the affection of his heavenly Father to ask the best for those who pray in his name. And because Jesus speaks for us, the Father who loves him treats us with affection out of love for his own child. It is as though a prince makes an appeal before his father, the king, for the good of a pauper. Though the king may have little cause to care for the pauper, because the son he loves makes the request, the king grants the pauper what he seeks.

Not only does Christ's intercession grant us spiritual paupers the ability to have our appeals lovingly heard by the Father, Jesus' continuing work grants us direct access to the Father. By his death, resurrection, and intercession, Christ Jesus enables us to approach our God and petition him as though we were the royal prince that he is. When we approach our God in Jesus' name, we have his own status as a child of the King. Christ continues to plead not only for our desires but also for our souls. He asks God to forgive our present sins and to apply his own righteousness to our account. The result is that, though we are fallen creatures, before God we have the holy status of Jesus himself.

Despite our sins, faults, and weaknesses, we enter the heavenly Father's throne room of grace on the basis of Christ's merit and his willingness to identify with us. Thus we pray "in Jesus' name" in praise of Christ's sacrifice and in recognition that our union with him alone gives us privileged access to the Father (Eph. 2:18–19).

The Power of Jesus' Name

With this access to the Father comes the privilege of praying with the blessing of the Holy Spirit. The role of the Holy Spirit is to make the name of Jesus known and to advance his kingdom (John 15:26–16:14). When we pray in Jesus' name, we are appealing to the Holy Spirit to conform our prayers to Christ's purposes.

The Spirit has no more pressing business than advancing the name of Jesus. So when we pray in Jesus' name, we are summoning the power of the Holy Spirit to accomplish his purposes. Any prayer truly offered in Jesus' name automatically engages the primary interest of the third person of the Trinity, who was (and remains) the power that moves the world—and everything in it.

By engaging this Spirit through the use of Jesus' name, we are also acknowledging the limits of our wisdom. The Spirit of God is infinitely wise and knows what our prayers should be. That is why the apostle Paul says that though we may not understand how to pray, the Holy Spirit intercedes to bring our prayers "in accordance with God's will" (Rom. 8:26–27). By praying in Jesus' name, we engage the power and the wisdom of the Holy Spirit. The result is that "in all things God works for the good of those who love him" (v. 28). We will explore these dynamics much more in later chapters, but for now it is important to recognize that praying in Jesus' name is an awesome privilege whereby we declare our honor of and dependence on the work of the three persons of the Trinity.

The Purpose of Jesus' Name

As great as is the privilege of praying "in Jesus' name," we will not know the full blessings of praying this way if we do not know the purpose of prayers that use these words. Throughout the Bible persons use the name of God to indicate that fulfilling his purposes is their highest priority. All that is done in God's name is for *his* glory. When Abraham, the father of the covenant people, claims land for the nation of God, he calls on the name of the Lord (Gen. 21:33). When the Old Testament people of God go forth to battle, they fight in his name (2 Chron. 14:11). Priests minister "in the name of the Lᴏʀᴅ" (Deut. 18:7). Prophets speak and act "in the name of the Lᴏʀᴅ" (v. 22; 1 Kings 18:32). David fought Goliath "in the name of the Lᴏʀᴅ" (1 Sam. 17:45). When God's people use his name, they indicate that they are seeking to bring honor to him. Whoever claims God's name declares the intention to serve his purposes.

The Old Testament pattern of service in God's name continues in the New Testament. Jesus comes in the name of the Lord (Matt. 23:39). In the name of Jesus, demons are cast out and miracles performed (Acts 16:18). The apostles exhort the church "in the name of the Lord" (1 Cor. 1:10). The church assembles "in the name of our Lord" (5:4). The church prays in the name of the Lord and is prayed for in the same way so that God might be glorified in all that his people do (Eph. 5:20; Col. 3:17).

To do anything in the Lord's name means to do it for his purposes. When we pray in Jesus' name, we are petitioning God to bring glory to Jesus and we are asking for his will to be done in everything so that he will be honored above all. Prayers in Jesus' name are enveloped with concern that he be represented, blessed, and glorified. By appealing to Jesus' name, we surrender our prayers to his purposes. This means that, while we should present many kinds of petitions to God, a prayer offered in Jesus' name ultimately requests his desires.

Praying in His Name—Always

Have you listened to the things children ask for when they pray? Children may request a new pony, a red bicycle, a win for their team, or that Mom will not discover the broken vase. Whose purposes are served if these prayers are answered? They seek the ultimate benefit of the child, not the glory of the Savior. They are offered for the child's sake rather than in Jesus' name.

Were we to pray backwards literally, we might be surprised to find how childish many of our prayers are:

- In Jesus' name, give me a new car.
- In Jesus' name, lower my taxes.
- In Jesus' name, make my stock go up in value.
- In Jesus' name, help me get out of this marriage.
- In Jesus' name, make my church get really big.

While there may be God-honoring purposes in some of these prayers, the glory of Jesus' name is not the primary focus of most of them. When we become the primary focus of our prayers and our earthly satisfaction is our greatest concern, then ending our prayer with Jesus' name is superfluous at best and possibly little more than superstition.

When we pray backwards, we are faced with the fact that Jesus' desires should be honored preeminently and ultimately, because he who bought us at the price of his own precious blood should have his purposes honored most highly. Praying backwards helps clarify the priorities of our prayers so that we can distinguish childish from mature petitions:

- Children pray, "Lord, give me what I want"; the mature pray, "Lord, conform me to what *you* want."
- Children pray for the fulfillment of their desires; the mature pray for the fulfillment of the Savior's purposes.
- Children pray for the things they can see; the mature pray that God will be seen.

26

- Children pray, "My will be done"; the mature pray, "Thy will be done."

The principles of praying backwards do not require us always to say the words "in Jesus' name" prior to our personal petitions. While there is nothing wrong with such a practice, it is not a magic formula or a secret password. Praying backwards is an attitude of the heart. To pray backwards means we back away from making ourselves, our wishes, or our wants the primary concerns of our prayer. We always put the purposes of Jesus first. We echo in heart if not in actual words the attitude of the psalmist who prayed, "Not to us, O LORD, not to us but to your name be the glory" (Ps. 115:1).

His Glory, Our Joy

One day not too long ago, I went to the hospital to visit my friend Eric, who was dying of a brain tumor. Months of fighting the cancer with chemo and prayer had seemed futile. I came to encourage Eric and had no idea how powerful his ministry would be to me. In that yellow-tiled room, lined with monitors and tubes that measured and maintained his life, Eric showed me the treasures of an eternal life that was his greater reality and glory.

I did not know how rough this beloved teacher's day had been until I entered his room. His head was hurting so much that he was dizzy with the pain. He grimaced when he smiled to greet me, and we said little as I put a hand on his shoulder. His wife smiled gratefully and rose to let me have her seat beside the bed. Seeing her vibrant, always exuberant husband in so much pain had been hard on her that day. She went into the hallway to cry and to let go of the brave face that she usually kept in place for him.

Eric spoke earnestly in the few minutes that she was gone. "Bryan," he said, "please help my family not to hurt too much.

I feel sorry for all of you. I will see Jesus soon, but you have to wait. I just pray that I can glorify the Lord through this."

I continue to marvel at this faith in God's eternal provision, and I continue to seek the depth of faith evident in Eric's prayer. In the midst of great suffering, he offered a simple petition: "In my life, Lord, be glorified." Of course, Eric desired the return of his physical health. Without question, he ached about the future of his young family. Eric put it all before the Lord in prayer, but Eric also ended his prayers, "In Jesus' name." That means that this faithful believer's greatest desire was to have his life—and, if necessary, his death—honor the name of his Savior.

I would not pretend to tell you that I know why Eric's dying rather than his living was more glorifying to God. Part of my heart still struggles to make sense of the loss of my friend. Yet this courageous man helped me to see, and wanted the world to know, that the God who loves us enough to sacrifice his own Son for us desired only the best for Eric, his family, and all the world that was touched by his life (Rom. 8:32). Eric was suffering in a fallen world where such experiences are common. Yet he had hope in a better world that many have yet to claim. If God could use Eric's faith in a time of suffering to display to many (including you who are reading this) the reality and security of that better world (2 Cor. 4:17–18), then Eric was most blessed—fulfilled in his greatest desire. Because of the wonders of his Lord's eternal provisions, Eric knew that "our present sufferings are not worth comparing with the glory that will be revealed in us" (Rom. 8:18). God was revealing his glory in Eric, and that was precisely Eric's desire.

Eric taught us all to pray, "God, you know my needs and my wants. They are plain to you and I ask you to provide for them. But, Lord, I love you so much that this is my ultimate prayer: Let my life be used to show the greatness and goodness of my God and his eternal love no matter what I face. Above all, I pray for the glory of Jesus' name." This is the essence and beauty of praying backwards.

In the strength that many of us have taken from Eric's example, I know that his prayer to glorify God has been answered. Still, it would be cruel and deceptive for any of us this side of heaven to give precise reasons for God's acts. His wisdom is far above ours and his plans beyond our fathoming (Rom. 11:33). Yet if the attitude undergirding every prayer is for the name of our God to be glorified, we need not doubt that he will answer according to his perfect will. And what more could we ask or desire than that God's will be fulfilled—the will of the One who loved us so much he gave us Jesus? When he gives us his best, we are most blessed.

Were it not for the witness of the cross, this trust in our God's intimate affection and ultimate purposes could seem to be empty fantasizing in the face of difficulties that baffle and buffet. Yet our trust in God is based not on our circumstances but on his character. God's display of his infinite love in the sacrifice of his Son assures us of his sovereign and eternal care. Jesus' suffering, death, and resurrection prove God's purposes are not thwarted by pain, and his affection is not exhausted by our experiences on this earth. The fulfillment of the will of such a God is always the greatest desire of those who know how infinite and wise is his love.

When we perceive the greatness and goodness of our God, our prayers become not so much a seeking after God for our purposes but an offering of ourselves for *his* purposes. We seek to offer no prayer to him that we could not pray backwards. In putting Jesus' name first, we move our designs to the rear and place his in the front of our affections. We offer our prayers with confidence not in our wisdom but in his, with priority not on our confused desires but on his perfect will, not for the glory of our name but in Jesus' name. Such commitment springs from the faith that when we pray in Jesus' name, he will give us the desires of our heart because our heart's greatest joy will be for his will to be done. We seek to have all our prayers and all that is in them honor the name of our infinitely wise, powerful, and loving Savior, knowing that when he is most honored, we are most blessed.

Key Thought: We can be sure that the prayers we offer are truly according to Christ's instruction not by following any verbal formula but by testing the motives of our heart. Even if we do not actually verbalize Jesus' name first, we should commit never to pray a prayer that we could not pray backwards.

Praying in Jesus' Name

Heavenly Father,

I pray to you today in Jesus' name.
Focus my heart on the priorities of my Savior,
    whom you have provided
      out of your great love.
Please do in me and through me whatever will
    bring most glory to Jesus.
As you listen to each petition I make,
    please help me offer it:
        claiming Christ's merit
          more than my own,
        seeking Christ's purposes
          more than my own,
        loving Christ's glory
          more than my own.
These are the petitions I offer:
(Offer your petitions here.)

By the power and wisdom of the Holy Spirit,
    transform my requests into instruments
    for accomplishing your will to have Christ
    honored everywhere—especially in my
    heart.
Make my greatest desire, highest joy, and
    deepest fulfillment Jesus' glory.
I can attempt all you require of my life,
      face all you design for my path,
        rejoice in all you will for my eternity,
    when I know all is for Jesus' name.
Do all that you know is best for him,
    for this most blesses me.
Forgive my readiness to forget
    and my tendency to doubt
    that when he is most glorified,
    I am most satisfied.
When my mind shrinks from these truths,
    enlarge my heart for Christ's purposes.
For Christ's sake and for mine,
    help me always to pray
In Jesus' name, amen.

2

Praying in Jesus' Way

Not My Will but Yours

Some years ago I faced a great challenge requiring intense focus and loads of emotional energy. For months I woke up with a lengthy list of tasks to do and people to contact. Long days were packed with phone calls, correspondence, meetings, and trips—and I dreaded most of them. Yet for all the invested effort, I had no clue if the outcome would be good or bad. My reputation and career were in jeopardy as well as the welfare of the many people for whom I am responsible as the leader of an institution. Scary times!

I would love to tell you I had a great prayer plan for each of those stressful days, but I cannot. When I tried to pray, my thoughts chased all the things that I needed to do. I wanted to meditate on the goodness of God, but my mind filled with the noise of surrounding expectations and occasional accusations. Though I knew the old saying "When it's hardest to pray, pray hardest," I could not find enough quietness within my soul to focus my prayers. *I could not pray as hard as I wanted.* Then I rediscovered the Lord's Prayer.

As a child, I learned the prayer that Jesus taught his disciples. I have recited it so many times that it can run out of my mouth and hardly tax my brain—or touch my heart. But one day the Lord let my eyes stumble across an account of a great man of God in circumstances similar to mine who focused on God by reciting the Lord's Prayer out loud as he took his morning walks. I am a jogger. I reasoned that if I could say this familiar prayer out loud on my morning run, then perhaps my other prayers would move forward too. I am from a church tradition that is not fond of repetitious prayer, but I was desperate.

So I began reciting the prayer as I ran. I am sure that other joggers, noticing my mumbling, thought a crazy person had joined them. There were still many times that I had trouble making my brain move through the prayer. Thoughts of tasks and strategies would still cut me off in midphrase before I realized what had happened. But then, because I knew the prayer so well, I could always pick up the line and force my brain to pray as Jesus taught. The result was that, despite all the distractions, I have never experienced a sweeter, richer time of prayer.

As I wrenched my mind from the daily turmoil and repeated the words of my Savior, the Holy Spirit began to minister to my heart. I found fresh comfort in the old phrases I had stopped really hearing. Yes, there were days when I still lost focus. At times I could not help but liken myself to the monk who is reputed to have wagered with a fellow monk whether either could recite the Lord's Prayer without being distracted. The second monk offered a horse to the first if he could recite the Lord's Prayer even once without his thoughts straying. The first monk took the bet and began to recite. Within two sentences he stopped and said, "You win. Even as I was praying, I began to wonder if the horse came with a saddle."

I know that kind of distraction, but I also know the mercy of my Lord who forgives my wayward thoughts and gives me his prayer to help keep my mind and heart riveted to him.

The Lord's Prayer

When we pray in Jesus' name, we petition God to fulfill the purposes of his kingdom and bring him glory. This is the way Jesus taught us to pray in his Sermon on the Mount. Three years later, when the disciples ask Jesus again to teach them to pray, he abbreviates the words of his first lesson but adds more explanation with parables. We will look at Christ's later teaching in this chapter and explore the added explanations here and in subsequent chapters.

In the abbreviated form of the Lord's Prayer, Jesus preserves the phrases that make plain the spiritual priorities of prayer that is offered in his name:

> Father, hallowed be your name,
> your kingdom come.
> Give us each day our daily bread.
> Forgive us our sins,
>   for we also forgive everyone who sins against us.
> And lead us not into temptation.
>
> Luke 11:2–4

Each petition of this model prayer has a different emphasis, but all teach the priorities that should dominate our thoughts when we pray in Jesus' name.

Make Your Name Holy

The first petition of the Lord's Prayer is, "Father, hallowed be your name." The words sound like a declaration of God's holiness in our way of speaking, but Jesus actually phrases these words as a request. He asks God to reverence or hallow his own name. By requesting that God honor his name, Jesus teaches us to ask God to make all creation recognize and revere his holiness. Of course, included in creation is the one praying. So in the same breath that we request God to make his name holy everywhere else, we also ask God to make our own heart honor him.

By praying, "hallowed be your name," we make God's holiness our highest priority and ask him to promote his glory in, around, and through us. Thus the first petition of the Lord's Prayer asks that all creation reverence God and that God exercise his will in ways that will advance his name in all the earth. The petition for God to hallow his name asks God to fulfill his righteous purposes for his glory.

Bring Your Kingdom

The second petition echoes the concern for God's honor that we seek in the first. Here, however, Jesus emphasizes God's honor as our heavenly King. The words "your kingdom come" ask God so to rule that his kingdom's purposes are fulfilled on earth.

In this petition, we essentially say to God, "May you have dominion. Rule over all things, great and small. Make your priorities determine the desires and acts of everyone in the world." With this kingdom request, Jesus reminds us to look toward the day when he will return and perfectly redeem this fallen world. But we are not simply to pray for the future kingdom of God. In the Lord's Prayer we express the desire for God to bring honor to his name every day and everywhere.

When he taught the Lord's Prayer the first time, Jesus explained the meaning of praying "your kingdom come" when he added "your will be done" (Matt. 6:10). By praying "your kingdom come," we are asking God for his will to be done "on earth as it is in heaven." Jesus' model for prayer places God's purposes as the highest priority of our petitions. This does not rule out prayers for our concerns but places them in proper order—secondary to his.

Provide Daily Bread

The third petition narrows the focus of our prayer. Moving from the vast kingdoms of heaven and earth, Jesus teaches us to pray very personally: "Give us each day our daily bread." The Lord does not tell us to request strawberry shortcake à la mode, though he is certainly capable of providing such pleasures. By urging us to pray for daily bread, Jesus teaches us another profound truth to fuel our faith.

Most people understand the prayer for daily bread to be a request for God to provide for our necessities—not necessarily our wants (such as strawberry shortcake à la mode). We need this understanding to caution those who think their Savior guarantees diamond rings and money trees. This instruction to pray for "necessities," however, should not shortchange other passages that encourage seeking "the desires of your heart" (Ps. 37:4). Our "wants" are not off the table in the Bible's prayer priorities. Rather, the Bible tells us to orient our wants so that both our heart and God's will be most fulfilled.

Psalm 37, which says God gives "the desires of your heart," begins with the command, "Delight yourself in the LORD." When we delight most in fulfilling his purposes (having his name reverenced and his kingdom furthered), then God gives us the desires of our heart. However, when we try to nourish our heart with empty pleasures or self-destructive pursuits, then the prayer for daily bread actually becomes a petition for a healthier diet. We ask God to feed our souls with heavenly fare.

A letter attributed to a Civil War soldier expresses God's prayer priorities and the ultimate desires of the heart shaped by the Holy Spirit:

I asked God for strength, that I might achieve.
   I was made weak, that I might humbly learn to obey.
I asked for health, that I might do greater things.
   I was given infirmity, that I might do better things.
I asked for riches, that I might be happy.
   I was given poverty, that I might be wise.
I asked for power, that I might have the praise of men.
   I was given weakness, that I might feel the need of God.
I asked for all things, that I might enjoy life.
   I was given life, that I might enjoy all things.
I got nothing that I asked for, but everything that I hoped
   for.
   Almost despite myself, my unspoken prayers were
   answered.
I among all men am most richly blessed.[1]

This record of the discovery of true blessing reminds us that Jesus designed the Lord's Prayer to reveal his desire to give us more fully, graciously, and suitably the very things we most want but mistakenly seek elsewhere. He does not want to deny us our desires but helps remove the false objects of our affections so that we will have the greater blessings he longs to lavish on us.

The prayer for daily bread reminds us of God's provision of manna in the wilderness. Israel's daily bread dropped from heaven to sustain them during deprivation. Over time, however, the people got tired of the manna. They grumbled about it and dreamed of their version of strawberry shortcake. Their sin was not in desiring tastier bread but rather in not appreciating the God who sustained them. They wanted bread that would make them less dependent on him and less devoted to his purposes. God's people were no longer most pleased by that which most glorified him.

The prayer for daily bread reorients us to God's purposes. With such prayer, we petition God to provide our greatest satisfaction through the things that he determines will most glorify him in our lives. Thus the prayer for daily bread is not just a request for boring whole wheat. We pray that God will provide all that is best for us and in so doing sustain our faith. This may be whole wheat or it may be strawberry shortcake. A prayer for daily bread does not limit God to the ordinary but petitions him to provide all that enables us to glorify him most. The prayer for daily bread is really a petition for spiritual vitality to do heaven's work on earth.

This spiritual provision may not always include physical food or the gifts that most please our natural desires. No concerns are greater to God than our greatest necessities. Ordinarily God supplies our needs with the regular provision of physical nourishment and the common blessings of our labors and loves. Every breath we take, every meal we eat, every piece of clothing we wear is an answer to the prayer for daily bread. The most ordinary, regular, and frequent answer to prayers for daily bread is God's faithful provision for our physical necessities. Most of the time God also provides far more than our necessities through the successes of our jobs, the relationships of our families, and the innumerable joys of our lives. Sometimes, however, God has a greater purpose in mind.

Faithful believers have sometimes starved and been denied the staples of life—comfort, security, health, and breath itself (Heb. 11:33–39). In the year 2000, human rights organizations reported that a radical Muslim regime in Sudan targeted Christians for mandatory conversion or extermination. The government allowed selective starvation and bombing of villages to force Christians to deny their faith. Most remained faithful, so the government undertook a more direct method of conversion. Christians were taken in groups of fifty many miles into the desert. Our brothers and sisters in Christ were then left without food or water. Every few days government trucks would return to the site with offers to rescue those who were ready to renounce their faith. The trucks would keep returning with the offer until there were no more Christians living. Then the trucks would bring the next group of fifty. The horror that continues in other forms in the Sudan and other parts of the world is beyond the ability of North American Christians truly to fathom. None of us questions whether these Sudanese Christians are faithful, but we may question whether God provided their daily bread, unless we understand that he does not limit his blessings to material provision.

In the midst of their suffering, our Sudanese brothers and sisters have had a deeper understanding than most of us of Christ's willingness to endure suffering for our eternal security. With a whisper or a blink, Jesus could have escaped all of his passion, yet he endured for us. The Sudanese believers understand better than I how precious is Jesus' gift, and as they give their lives, they teach us of greater joys than the world can provide or deny. As a result, Christians around the world are inspired to greater faithfulness for the sake of their witness to millions more who need the spiritual nourishment of our Savior.

Suffering proves neither that someone has been faithless nor that God has failed to provide daily bread. Jesus assures us that those who follow him will sometimes face suffering and death (John 15:20). In fact, until he returns, we will all die. This does not mean that everyone abandons prayer in old age or that God stops listening to the elderly. God always answers the prayer for daily bread by providing for our greatest needs. Those needs, however, are not always physical and material. Jesus said, "Man does not live on bread alone, but on every word that comes from the mouth of God" (Matt. 4:4). The most important things in life are those which nourish our relationship with the God of eternal life. God will always provide this bread to those who seek him (John 6:32–35, 41–58).

To deepen our faith and to make us greater witnesses of the spiritual realities and comforts of eternity, God may have to deny physical blessings in this life. In doing so he never denies the "daily bread" he teaches us to seek in the Lord's Prayer. Jesus taught us precisely the nature of this fare when he said, "My food . . . is to do the will of him who sent me" (John 4:43). The Christian who prays for daily bread asks God to supply the food necessary to further his eternal purposes. For the one who delights in doing God's will, there is no greater nourishment or pleasure than this daily bread.

When the Holy Spirit renews our heart supernaturally, our greatest longing is to be and do all that God desires (Rom. 8:5). When Christians pray for daily bread, we are not simply praying for our natural wants. We are praying for the ability to please God, because pleasing God satisfies us. A missionary of retirement age chose to return to the field. "Don't you want to take some time to enjoy yourself?" she was asked. "Oh," she replied, "don't worry about me. At this stage of my life, I do whatever I want." But then with a twinkle in her eye she added, "But I want most to please God."

Heaven's bread is God's supply of everything we need to nourish the desire and ability to please him. The prayer for daily bread is but another way of saying to God, "May your will be done in my life."

Keep from Temptation

The request for daily bread and the other petitions that follow use thoughts from the book of Proverbs. There Solomon petitions God for daily bread so that he will be kept from temptation: "Keep falsehood and lies far from me; give me neither poverty nor riches, but give me only my daily bread. Otherwise, I may have too much and disown you and say, 'Who is the LORD?' Or I may become poor and steal, and so dishonor the name of my God" (Prov. 30:8–9).

Jesus' use of this ancient passage makes it clear that his prayer for daily bread is about more than physical food. The Old Testament prayer for daily bread comes in the context of a believer asking to be kept from temptation. He asks to

41

be spared from poverty, not simply because it is unpleasant but because it may tempt him to steal and dishonor God. At the same time, the prayer asks God to keep him from owning so many treasures that pride and material preoccupation would cause him to disown God. In this nation of great affluence where God's hand is so easily denied and the underprivileged so easily forgotten, we should well understand this temptation.

The ancient writer petitions heaven to keep him from the temptations that come with either poverty or wealth. He wants only that all forms of temptation be kept distant and asks only for the provision of daily bread—not more and not less. He realizes that the provision of daily bread enables him to fulfill rather than counter God's purposes. Thus the prayer for daily bread naturally flows into the petition "Lead us not into temptation." By granting the earlier petition, God provides the means to fulfill the latter one. And in combination, both petitions guard the spiritual health of believers and orient their lives toward fulfilling God's will.

Jesus does not pray with the expectation that God would ever tempt us. The Bible teaches: "When tempted, no one should say, 'God is tempting me.' For God cannot be tempted by evil, nor does he tempt anyone" (James 1:13). Instead, we are tempted when selfish priorities and evil desires cause us to forsake the will of God (v. 14). The trials God uses to build up our faith Satan tries to hijack and use as temptations to tear down our spiritual commitment. In this sense, the very same circumstance can be a nurturing instrument from God's heart *and* an injurious temptation in Satan's hand. Ultimately the key to whether a circumstance is a trial or a temptation is not found in its features but in our heart. The Lord's Prayer teaches us to pray that God, who knows the capabilities of our heart, would keep from us anything that Satan could use to overpower our ability to do God's will.

The pinnacle purpose of our prayers remains constant: being enabled to do the will of God for the glory of God. "Lead us not into temptation" is a crisp way of saying, "Lord, keep us from acting in ways that would prevent us from honoring you. Keep us from being tempted by not having our needs met, and take from us preoccupation with our wants. Erase from our lives anything that would tempt us to dishonor you." When we pray for rescue from temptation, we ask God to make his will our desire—to dominate our thoughts and actions with divine purpose. Therefore the prayer for God not to lead us into temptation includes automatically our request for him to enable us to desire and do his will.

Forgive

Not only does Christ teach us to pray for protection from personal temptation, but he also instructs us in the way to return to honoring God when we yield to temptation—and when others do. Jesus teaches us to pray, "Forgive our sins." These three words open the door to the vast storehouse of heaven's mercy. To give us the right to utter these words, Jesus gave his life. He shed his blood to pay the penalty for the sin of all who trust in him. Now, whoever asks for pardon in his name receives God's mercy forever. The more we desire to honor the Lord who loves us so, the more we recognize our constant need of his grace. Jesus' willingness to teach these words as a regular pattern for our prayers greatly encourages us, because we know that we will not exhaust his mercy.

Regardless of the degree or frequency of our sin, we can ask forgiveness. In fact, by praying as Jesus taught, we acknowledge both that sin sifts into our lives and that his grace is great enough to secure our pardon. Our prayers for forgiveness not only confess the weakness in our nature but also honor the grace in his. Both aspects of the petition for forgiveness reorient our life to God's will and cause us to reflect more of his character.

The concern to reflect the character of God revealed in our request for pardon naturally unfolds into a commitment to forgive others. Jesus teaches us to pray, "Forgive us . . . , for we also forgive everyone who sins against us." Perfectly fulfilling the second part of this petition must *not* be considered a condition of the first. If God pardons us only after we have rightly, adequately, or fully forgiven those who sin against us, then no one would ever have God's full pardon.

The story is told of a minister who once heard a sea captain bark orders to his crew, saying, "And if you fail, pray that God will forgive you, because I will not." The minister replied to the captain, "Then I pray that you will never sin, because the Lord's Prayer teaches that we are forgiven in the same way that we forgive others." The minister's response sounds very brave and spiritual, but if it were true, we would all stand condemned before God. We are not able to forgive in the same way that God forgives us. We have too little ability to erase our memories and too much resentment etched in our hearts for Jesus to make God's pardon of us dependent on our pardon of others. Our forgiveness is never as complete or compassionate as his. Tiny seeds of bitterness still sprout—sometimes quite unexpectedly—from soil we thought we had weeded of all bitterness. Only the faith that God fully pardons all that we can never fully correct (including the unforgiveness in our heart) makes our pardon sure. And the sureness of his unconditional pardon makes his mercy our own compulsion. When we have truly understood how great is God's love for us—though we, by our sin, have abused his care and trampled on the blood of his Son—then our hearts soften toward those who have wronged us. This is why Jesus' prayer makes our forgiveness of others a necessary consequence and a personal confirmation of our reception of his grace rather than a condition of our request for forgiveness.

Were Jesus to teach us to pray, "Lord, forgive us as much as we forgive others or only when we have forgiven others adequately," then we would always have reason to worry. Jesus, however, teaches us to pray, "Lord, forgive our sin, for—*in your doing so*—we also forgive everyone who sins against us."

Experiencing the greatness and grace of his pardon warms our heart and makes us long to please him. As a consequence, we reflect his nature and become more and more like him. His pardoning nature becomes more of our nature so that his will for others becomes more our desire for them—even those who sin against us.

Jesus teaches us to approach our heavenly Father with the humility to ask, "Lord, let me not only know your forgiveness but radiate it." Jesus wants to express the glories of his grace to us and through us. When we grasp his intent, then we understand that asking for personal forgiveness automatically creates an obligation and compulsion to forgive. You simply cannot truly experience grace without having it profoundly transform your attitude toward others. As baby bottles filled with warm milk cannot help but become warm, hearts warmed by Christ's grace cannot but become gracious. The radiating warmth of God's grace may take time and prayer, but then that is why Jesus taught us to pray this way regularly. His will is to have his grace constrain our will to be like his.

A Golden Thread

The petitions of the Lord's Prayer are not a string of unrelated requests. While each petition has a specific focus, all have a common purpose. The golden thread that knits the petitions together is the seeking of God's will.

Each petition provides a way of saying to God in every circumstance, "Your will be done." This is not a perfunctory turning from our selfish interests to please or appease God. The petition for God's will to be done is the greatest desire of hearts indwelt by God's Spirit. Our hearts are designed to find their greatest joy in honoring the God who loves us infinitely.

Not only does Jesus teach us to pray with a surpassing love for heaven's purposes, he prayed the same way. Though he came from heaven as the perfect God-man, the human aspect of his being understandably recoiled from the crushing pain to come in his crucifixion. Jesus petitioned his heavenly Father to "take this cup from me." With faithfulness to his divine nature and to us, Jesus also prayed, "yet not my will, but yours be done" (Luke 22:42).

By his example as well as by the instruction of the Lord's Prayer, Jesus teaches us to undergird every request with: "Yet not my will, Lord, but your will be done." In essence, Jesus teaches us again to pray backwards. We put his purposes first, because we treasure his honor above our earthly desires.

Our traditions keep us praying, "In Jesus' name," at the conclusion of our prayers. The Bible also tells us to pray in Jesus' name; however, it does not say where to include the phrase or even the precise words to use (see, for example, Eph. 5:20). Perhaps the reason for the Bible's lack of specific direction is that the name of Jesus is the fountain, as well as the foundation, of every petition we offer when we pray as he taught us. Faithful prayer begins with, ends with, and consists of the desire to honor our Savior.

I am not advocating the overthrow of long-standing and helpful habits. Perfectly fine and proper prayers close with the words "in Jesus' name." However, we have the privilege of bathing all of our prayer in the name of our Savior. Instead of mindlessly tacking on "in Jesus' name" at the end out of habit, every petition can be and should be offered to bring him glory. We have the joy of knowing that we can pray to further the purposes of the God who loves us. As a result, the glory of the name that we love above all names becomes the aim of our every prayer and the promised end. When we make his will the preeminent desire of our prayer, then we not only end our prayer in Jesus' name, but we also have the assurance that he will glorify his name in us.

Before confronting the terrorists who had commandeered Flight 93 on September 11, 2001, Todd Beamer prayed the

Lord's Prayer with a GTE Airfone operator. Surely Todd did not want to die. When he prayed with the operator on the ground, his heart must have longed for physical rescue. He must have wanted and prayed to see his wife and children again. But with the Lord's Prayer, he prayed for something greater. Through the prayer that had been resident in his spirit since his childhood days, Todd prayed for God's name to be hallowed, for God's kingdom to come, for daily bread, for freedom from temptation—and for the forgiveness of himself and others. In essence, Todd prayed for God's will to be done. That's why he prayed in Jesus' name.

Todd's wife, Lisa, explains, "I don't think that Todd chose to die, but he did choose for God's will to be done in his life. Knowing that, he stepped into the aisle of the plane, trusting by faith that regardless of what happened, God would be true to his Word."[2] Many in the world—perhaps many reading these words—will not understand how God could be "true to his Word" and let this faithful husband, father, and hero die. The answer is that God glorified his name in Todd. From his earliest days, Todd had trusted Jesus to forgive his sins and secure his eternity. Todd was able to risk his life for many, because he knew that his eternal life was secure with his Savior. What Jesus did for Todd, and enabled Todd to do for many, glorifies the name of Jesus.

Lisa adds, "Todd was not a Hollywood hunk or a comic-book superhero. He was an ordinary guy with ordinary faith in a great God." Todd did *not* get the answer to the prayer for physical safety that he must have offered, but he received precisely what his faith requested in the Lord's Prayer. Todd asked for God's will to be done, and in his witness to the world of the greatness and goodness of his God, Todd fulfilled the greatest desires of his heart. He glorified the One in whose name he prayed.

Key Thought: Jesus teaches us to undergird every prayer with the foundational petition, "Yet not my will, Lord, but your will be done." In essence, Jesus is teaching us to pray backwards. We put his purposes first when we treasure his honor above all our earthly desires. Ultimately this is no sacrifice on our part, because we know that through our Savior's answers, we will be most blessed.

Praying in Jesus' Way

Most holy and gracious God,
We offer this prayer of Christ, through Christ,
    to Christ, and for his eternal glory:
Our Father in heaven,
Hallowed be your name,
Your kingdom come, your will be done
    on earth as it is in heaven.
Give us today our daily bread.
Forgive us our debts,
    as we also have forgiven our debtors.
And lead us not into temptation,
    but deliver us from evil;
for yours is the kingdom and the power and the
    glory forever.
Amen.

From Romans 11:36 and Matthew 6:9–13

3

Praying without Doubting

Trusting Our Father, the King

A
n old story tells of two widows who lived together in a cottage at the foot of a mountain. Soaking rains had loosened the soil on the mountain's slope, and a huge boulder threatened to roll onto their home. The two women remembered that Jesus taught if they had faith as a mustard seed, they could move mountains (Matt. 17:20). All the two wanted was for a piece of the mountain *not* to move. So they mustered up their faith and began to pray for God to anchor the stone. But it rolled down the mountain and crushed the cottage. Then one of the women admitted to the other: "I knew that the boulder was too big for our little prayer to work."

We, of course, do not expect a prayer offered in doubt to engage God's power. Jesus said, "I tell you the truth, if anyone says to this mountain, 'Go, throw yourself into the sea,' and does not doubt in his heart but believes that what he says will happen, it will be done for him. Therefore I tell you, whatever you ask for in prayer, believe that you have received it, and it will be yours" (Mark 11:23–24; see also Matt. 21:21).

But how are we supposed to pray without doubting? Is it wrong to allow any thought that we might not receive the answer we desire? If so, how do we keep negative thoughts from invading our brain? Isn't being told not to doubt a little like being told not to think about pink elephants? Once you have been told not to think about something, it's practically impossible not to think about it.

How can we even be sure that we're making the right requests? Only God understands the intricacies of creation and eternity. Since we do not possess the wisdom to anticipate all the consequences of our petitions, it seems arrogant—even dangerous—to demand that God do precisely what *we* want. In fact praying without any doubt would seem to require us to tell God what to do. And if millions of Christians all over the world are controlling God's will with their limited understanding and mixed motives, then what keeps the world from shattering into a zillion shards of personal priorities? Finally, if God's will is really under the control of my will, then wouldn't that make me God?

Believing Prayer

The Bible teaches us to believe in prayer without abandoning our beliefs about God and ourselves. Faithful prayer hinges on how we understand the terms *belief* and *doubt*. Well-meaning persons sometimes try to explain believing prayer with examples of persons who prayed that something would happen, expressed unwavering confidence that it would happen, and then watched it happen. It may be difficult to consider any alternative teaching, but when we weigh the consequences of making an infinitely wise God subject to our finite wisdom and human wants, then we must seek other descriptions of faithful prayer.

Pastor Ken Smith tells of a meeting with the head of a security company that shared office space with survivors of the 9/11 attack on the World Trade Center.[1] The survivors' company had been decimated by the attack. The survivors remained both grateful and troubled for the circumstances that separated them from the tragic deaths of their co-workers:

- The head of the company got in late that day because he wanted to be with a child starting kindergarten.
- Another man is alive because it was his turn to bring donuts.
- A woman survived because her alarm clock didn't go off in time.
- Another was delayed because of an accident on the New Jersey Turnpike.
- One missed his bus.
- One spilled food on her clothes and had to take time to change.
- One person's car wouldn't start.
- One went back to answer the telephone.
- A mother had a child who dawdled and didn't get ready as soon as he should have.
- A man with a new pair of shoes developed a blister. He stopped at a drugstore to buy a Band-Aid. That is why he is alive today.

If any of these persons were regularly praying Christians, they might have prayed for God to spare them the inconvenience of that morning. But the inconvenience spared their lives. Before we adopt a prayer philosophy that requires God to provide all our wants, we must adjust our thinking to consider the limitations of our understanding. In our finite wisdom, we may least want what an infinitely wise God will most bless!

Moving-Mountain Prayers

The basic problem with all definitions of believing prayer that make God the servant of our will is that the *object* of belief is misplaced. Proper belief is not unwavering confidence that something we want will happen, nor is it doubtless trust that we know what is best. Our trust is not in the thing that we want or in our sufficient faith. The success of our prayers does not lie in exceptional confidence that *we* have pumped enough of our own faith into our prayer (and extracted enough doubt) so that now God must respond. Our belief must be in God. He, not our desire, is the object of our faith.

We pray believing that God is all-powerful, all-wise, and infinitely loving—and that we are not. We tell God our desires for matters large and small, but always our greatest desire is that his will be done. We yield to God's will because we *believe* that the Good Shepherd will provide only the absolute best. Thus when Jesus teaches us to ask and we will receive (Luke 11:9–10), he does so only after telling us that those who believe in him ask for the will and purpose of God above all things (vv. 2–4). Praying in Jesus' name requires seeking first the kingdom of God and his righteousness with the absolute trust that God will then add all that is best for us (Matt. 6:31–33). This is the way that Jesus prayed and the way he taught us to pray (see chapters 1 and 2).

Escape-Hatch Prayers

Some people say that you are not praying with sufficient faith if you follow your petitions with, "Yet, Lord, not my will but your will be done." Others may claim you are hedging your bets or leaving yourself an escape hatch for explaining unanswered prayer. But do not let anyone make you feel guilty or ashamed for praying as Jesus did in the Garden of Gethsemane.

When Jesus asked for deliverance in the Garden, his prayer was so intense that sweat fell from him in drops of blood (Luke

22:44). He also prayed with full confidence that his sovereign Father was able to send twelve legions of angels to rescue him (Matt. 26:53). No one could accuse Jesus of praying with insufficient fervor or faith. Still, he said, "Yet, Lord, not my will but your will be done." Jesus was not expressing doubt because he prayed for God's will to be done. Our Savior was right both to offer his petition and to subject it to God's design. Seeking the will of his Father was the mark of Jesus' faithfulness, not the failure of it.

Prayer can be offered with a sacrosanct appeal to God's will that is little more than a cover for doubt in God's presence or prayer's power. Yet though faithless prayer can misuse words about bowing to God's will, faithful prayer means them.

We should not let anyone judge our heart when we pray as Jesus did, and as did one he healed. Early in the Savior's ministry, the leper who faithfully approached Jesus for healing said, "If you are willing, you can make me clean" (Mark 1:40).

In this brief but instructive petition, the leper states his trust that Jesus is able to heal at the same time he concedes that his health depends on Jesus' willingness to help. This recognition of the need for Christ's willingness to heal is not a concession of faith but an affirmation of it. We affirm similar faith when we pray, "Lord, I know that you can do all things. In my human wisdom I make this request, but you know the end from the beginning. Hear my prayer and do what you know is right. I entrust this to your will because I believe in your wisdom, power, and love." Such prayer is a far greater expression of faith than daring to stand before the throne of heaven, sidling up to God, and saying, "Lord, I know exactly what should happen; let's do this my way."

All who are so bold as to tell God exactly how to answer are expressing a kind of belief, but it is great faith in human wisdom and faint confidence in our God. I do not have the wisdom, insight, or vision to prescribe God's acts. I do not know whether I will take another breath after finishing this sentence, or if the one reading it will. My confidence and yours should rest not on our limited knowledge but on God's unfathomable wisdom, inestimable power, and unfailing love.

Aladdin's Lamp Prayers

How do we apply passages where Jesus says, "Whatever you ask in prayer, believe that you have received it, and it will be yours" (Mark 11:24)? To understand such statements, we must first remember that we are told to ask for all that promotes the will and glory of God.

Jesus qualifies his promise to give "whatever you ask in prayer" by the reminder that we should not expect God's favor if we hold grudges (vv. 25–26). Additionally, Christ's promise to honor our requests comes in the context of his demonstrating (through the cursing of a fig tree representing the Jewish leaders who rejected him) how he will deny blessing to anyone who refuses to give preeminent glory to God (vv. 11–23; see also Matt. 21:15–22). Jesus' promise to provide whatever we ask in prayer rests on the understanding that we will pray with godly priorities.

We cannot rip Mark 11:24 from its context to make Christian prayer an Aladdin's lamp for the fulfillment of self-serving wishes. In fact, if the primary focus of our prayer is to glorify ourselves and satisfy our earthly desires, then this passage promises Christ's judgment against our prayers. The consequences of selfish prayer are very serious. Perhaps this is why Jesus precedes this instruction on prayer with the caution *not* to put faith in our wisdom but to have faith in God (Mark 11:22).

Always there is a context for the verses that assure us God will answer whatever we request. Promises for answered prayer come with the understanding, and often the command, that our prayer should be offered in Jesus' name—for our Lord's purposes and to honor him:

- "And I will do whatever you ask in my name, so that the Son may bring glory to the Father. You may ask me for anything in my name, and I will do it" (John 14:13–14).

- "If you remain in me and my words remain in you, ask whatever you wish, and it will be given you" (15:7).
- "You did not choose me, but I chose you and appointed you to go and bear fruit—fruit that will last. Then the Father will give you whatever you ask in my name" (v. 16).
- "You do not have, because you do not ask God. When you ask, you do not receive, because you ask with wrong motives, that you may spend what you get on your pleasures" (James 4:2–3).
- "Dear friends, if our hearts do not condemn us, we have confidence before God and receive from him anything we ask, because we obey his commands and do what pleases him" (1 John 3:21–22).

These verses are not a blank check for our whims and wants. They are something better. They are God's assurance that when we seek him first, he will answer to glorify his Son. And because Jesus is most glorified when his wisdom, goodness, and greatness are most on display, these promises assure us that he will answer our prayers better than we can ask. We struggle to believe such a promise, but belief in God's intention to do such immeasurable good prompts faithful prayer that heaven delights to answer.

Believing in God's Sovereignty

To ensure God's responses to our prayers, we must believe he is able to answer. Jesus follows his teaching of the Lord's Prayer with this simple assurance: "Ask and it will be given to you; seek and you will find; knock and the door will be opened to you. For everyone who asks receives; he who seeks finds; and to him who knocks, the door will be opened" (Luke 11:9–10). The promises that God will answer those who ask, reveal to those who seek, and open to those who knock presume he is able to do as he says. When we say we believe God is all-powerful, all-knowing, and all-loving, so that he can do as he promises, we affirm his sovereignty. We could use many words to describe divine sovereignty, but it boils down to this: God is in control and we are not. He rules over all things to accomplish the purposes that most glorify him and most bless his people.

Failure to believe in God's sovereign power submarines our incentive to pray. Why would we pray to someone who cannot respond? Why would we ask God to take care of our greatest needs if he has neither the power, will, nor wisdom to do so? Jesus' simple assurance that everyone who asks receives encourages us to make requests of a God who can sovereignly provide all that he promises.

A God Who Abundantly Answers

Belief in God's sovereignty coupled with his promises to reward those who diligently seek him (Heb. 11:6) provides even more powerful incentive to pray. The confidence that he has the power to promote his glory and the love to provide for our good also enables us to face disappointments without doubting his eternal plan. We expect a God who is truly sovereign to answer prayers in ways beyond our wisdom. How else could he "do immeasurably more than all we ask or imagine" (Eph. 3:20)?

A young man I know began to preach in a small church soon after he professed his faith in Jesus. The fledgling minister did not know much about the Bible, people, or preaching. He just knew that God wanted others to know about Jesus. So the young man prayed and prayed that God would do "a mighty work" in that church, but the church did not flourish. Mistakes the well-intentioned but untrained pastor made in relationships and in teaching fractured the already fragile church. He left, and soon after, the church closed its doors.

Grief over people in that community living and dying without a church's care deepened the young man's desire for effective ministry. So, freed of the daily obligations of the small church, he pursued further training. Awareness of the needs he had left behind stirred the young man to study as diligently as any student I have ever had. Now, as a trained minister, he is one of the finest preachers I know.

In the little church God actually did the "mighty work" for which my friend prayed. There the Lord placed a talented servant on a path to great service. He simply needed to reach a dead end to know that he needed to look for the right road. The mighty work did not come as the young man expected, but in God's sovereign plan the pastor was led to serve more people than he would ever have touched in the remote church where his ministry began. God answered the minister's prayer beyond anything he had asked or imagined. Additionally, a few years later, another man who had trained under the ministry of this man of God returned to the pastor's original community and ministers very effectively there. The "mighty work" the first young pastor prayed for continues to be accomplished through God's sovereign care.

A God Who Always Answers

God always answers the prayer of faith. He delights to honor prayer that does not doubt him. When we pray believing that he will sovereignly work for our good and his glory, God always answers in absolutely the best way. Such prayer looks past the limitations of our earthly vision for heaven's answers. We freely acknowledge our disappointments when the promotion does not come, when we fail the test, when a child rebels, when injustice occurs, when relationships erode, when storms destroy, and when evil has its day. But faith clings to the certainty that the disappointment is due to the limitations of our human sight, because a sovereign God is able to accomplish much that is beyond our sight.

Faith in God's sovereignty actually causes us to rejoice that we do not bind God with the limited wisdom and mixed motives of our prayers. Who would want to live in a universe controlled by creatures as finite and fallible as we? We pray with the confidence that a sovereign God always answers our prayers. Because he is in control, he is able to incorporate his answers to our petitions into his perfect plan. God always answers in one of four ways: yes, no, not yet, or immeasurably more than all we ask or imagine.

God's sovereign oversight of our prayers assures us that we can seek him when we are struggling with life's greatest difficulties. We don't have to have the answers all figured out before we ask his help. He will provide the best even when—or especially when—we confess that we have more questions than answers about how to pray (Rom. 8:26). For instance, when we are struggling with serious illness, there are Bible passages that seem to promise more than we may feel that we have the right (or the faith) to ask. James exhorts us to pray for sick persons with this promise: "the prayer offered in faith will make the sick person well; the Lord will raise him up" (James 5:15). How can we offer such a prayer in faith when we know of faithful Christians with seriously ill loved ones? Begin by believing that God always answers this prayer too.

Lest you think that I have put God in a box and am proposing to put all doctors out of business, consider the careful wording of the Bible: "And the prayer offered in faith will make the sick person well; the Lord will raise him up. If he has sinned, he will be forgiven. Therefore confess your sins to each other and pray for each other so that you may be healed. The prayer of a righteous man is powerful and effective" (James 5:15–16). In the original language James says literally that the Lord will "save" (*sōzō*) the sick person and will "raise him up." The Bible uses these words elsewhere to refer to spiritual salvation and resurrection, not simply to physical healing (see Luke 19:10; 1 Cor. 1:21; 6:14; 2 Cor. 4:14; Heb. 7:25).

James makes the spiritual connection even clearer by including the command to confess sins as part of the process of praying for healing. God's ultimate purpose is to secure the eternal health of the one who is sick. Whether the illness is a consequence of unconfessed sin or unhealed disease, the ultimate aim of the healing prayer is the spiritual security of the sick person whom God will "save" and "raise up." Note that James promises not merely the healing of the disease through faithful prayer but also the healing of sin: "If he has sinned, he will be forgiven." James is preeminently concerned about *saving* (in the spiritual sense) the sick person.

Of course, the Lord can heal physical illness, and most of the time he does. I have not died of the many infections, genetic weaknesses, and accidents that are as typical of my life as they are yours. I have prayed for God to heal those stricken with disease, damaged in crashes, and endangered in delivery. After these prayers, God has healed many times. God commands us to pray for the sick, and most of the time he does heal. Every moment that my white corpuscles fend off disease, that my immune system staves off internal collapse, and that my path providentially takes me away from countless unseen catastrophes, God answers prayer for my well-being. God may use the natural processes of our body, the blessed insights of modern medicine, or the miraculous intervention of his Spirit to heal. Each is a blessing of his hand for those who understand that no medicine or miracle benefits us apart from his power.

A God beyond All Boundaries

While the most frequent and regular answer to healing prayer is physical rescue—through means both ordinary and extraordinary—the eternal God is not limited to the boundaries of this earth in his promise to heal. The omnipotent Lord has other options for healing that lie in the salvation and resurrection language of James's promise. Our Lord can heal us on this earth. Still, the healing that takes place in the Lord's time on this earth will leave our body imperfect. Our body will inevitably decay and we will die—until the day that our Lord returns to make this world and our body perfect. But God has an option beyond this imperfect healing of our temporal existence.

We are eternal beings. Our physical existence is neither the extent of our time nor the limit of God's opportunity to heal. God can also raise us to himself for the healing that is perfect and eternal. In his sovereign timing, he may choose to do this late or early in our measurement of life, because our earthly life span is but the blink of an eye in God's eternal time frame.

The Lord heals. He can perform the perfect healing of raising us up to immortality with him or the imperfect healing of repairing our mortal body on earth for a time. If the first option seems less remarkable to us, it is only because we have limited our assessment of the glorious to that which human eyes can see. Instead, the Bible gives us the eyes of faith—the ability to see that our heavenly existence is just as real, just as sure, and more glorious than the physical reality of our present world. We do not know precisely the details of our immortal existence, but the Bible assures us that, when Christ appears, "we shall be like him" (1 John 3:2). C. S. Lewis helps us relish this ultimate reality by saying that if we were allowed to see the persons nearest to us in the state of glory they will enjoy when Christ raises them, we would be tempted to fall down and worship them.

A God of Eternal Priorities

Among our loved ones are those who are suffering illnesses. Such afflictions will be with us until Christ comes and reclaims this broken world. Until that day it is good to pray for healing. As we have seen, most of the time God graciously grants healing through the wonders of the bodies he made and the wisdom of the physicians he provides. Still, these earthly provisions have limits. So we pray because we trust in God's sovereign providence. He may miraculously cure for a time, or he may hasten an eternal cure by raising a loved one to Christ's side. In either case, however, we trust that God is accomplishing his eternal purposes and our eternal good.

60

The last time noted pastor and author James Montgomery
Boice addressed his congregation before succumbing to cancer,
he spoke of the trust that healing prayer includes.

A relevant question, when you pray is, pray for what? Should
you pray for a miracle? Well you are free to do that, of course.
My general impression is that the God who is able to do miracles—and he certainly can—is also able to keep you from
getting the problem in the first place. So although miracles
do happen, they're rare by definition. A miracle has to be an
unusual thing.

. . . [P]ray for wisdom for the doctors. . . . [Pray] also for the
effectiveness of the treatment.

Above all I would say pray for the glory of God. If you think
of God glorifying himself in history and you say, where in all of
history has God most glorified himself? He did it at the cross
of Jesus Christ, and it wasn't by delivering Jesus from the cross,
though he could have. Jesus said, "Don't you think I could call
down from my Father ten legions of angels for my defense?" But
he didn't do that. And yet that's where God is most glorified.
. . .

When things like this come into our lives, they are not ac-
cidental. It's not as if God somehow forgot what was going
on, and something bad slipped by. . . . God does everything
according to his will. . . .

But what I've been impressed with most is something in addition to that. It's possible, isn't it, to conceive of God as sovereign
and yet indifferent? God's in charge, but he doesn't care. But it's
not that. God is not only the one who is in charge. God is also
good. Everything he does is good.

. . . [I]f God does something in your life, would you change
it? If you'd change it, you'd make it worse. It wouldn't be as good.
So that's the way we want to accept it and move forward, and
who knows what God will do?

"Sing to the Lord, all the earth, proclaim his salvation day
after day. Declare his glory among the nations, his marvelous

deeds among the peoples. For great is the Lord and most worthy of praise. . . ."[2]

Whenever physical healing does not occur and suffering is prolonged, we should not minimize the pain but remember its eternal frame. This affliction is but for a moment of our eternity and works in us and in others a dependence on Christ that makes heaven's promises surer and more precious. The apostle Paul writes:

> We know that the one who raised the Lord Jesus from the dead will also raise us with Jesus and present us with you in his presence. All this is for your benefit, so that the grace that is reaching more and more people may cause thanksgiving to overflow to the glory of God.
> Therefore we do not lose heart. Though outwardly we are wasting away, yet inwardly we are being renewed day by day. For our light and momentary troubles are achieving for us an eternal glory that far outweighs them all. So we fix our eyes not on what is seen, but on what is unseen.
>
> 2 Corinthians 4:14–18

Since this world presently holds the pain of our wasting away, we long all the more for the world where there are no more tears. And we treasure more the God who provides eternal life for us and for many more whom he draws to himself by such longing. He who holds our eternity in his hand sovereignly works all things so that even the misery of this broken world leads to the eternal security of those whose desperation guides them to union with him.

God has given us the perspective of Scripture to see the eternal plane on which he operates. The apostle Paul, who healed others miraculously, adopted this perspective when he prayed three times for the Lord to heal his thorn in the flesh. God did not remove the thorn, and Paul understood that the Lord was teaching him: "My grace is sufficient for you, for my power is made perfect in weakness" (2 Cor. 12:9).

Jesus had eternity in view when he faced the cross and asked for the withering pain to pass from him but only if this were God's will. With such a perspective, we are able to see that disease and suffering do not automatically reveal a failure of faith. Even death does not prove that God has failed. If we are temporally healed in this life, this is God's doing. If we are eternally healed by passing into heaven, this too is God's doing.

With faith in God's sovereignty over eternity undergirding our prayers, I have often encouraged others *not* to pray for God to heal *if* it is his will—as though maybe he will heal and maybe not. Instead, I encourage my friends and family to pray for God to heal *according* to his will. Then, whether he answers with the temporary healing that keeps a loved one with us longer, or whether he answers with the perfect healing of taking that one into Jesus' arms, we remain confident that he has blessed. We have faith that our God's blessings will be according to a sovereign plan that is as beautiful and boundless as he.

Disease and suffering are inevitable in our fallen world. Yet amid the hurt and confusion, we can pray without doubting that these afflictions are not the ultimate reality or the final chapter of King Jesus' response to the prayers of his people. Our Lord Jesus will use our prayer in his name to extend his rule through this world and the next. He is able because he is sovereign over all things for all time.

Seeing God's Sovereignty

Some time ago I needed to make a difficult financial announcement to the seminary I serve, and I was stewing about it during my early-morning jog in a neighborhood park. Deep in thought, I came to the top of a hill just as flying geese were approaching a nearby lake from the other side of the rise in preparation for their splash landing. The result was that for a split second I found myself face-to-face with a rapidly approaching goose. I ducked to my right, but he dodged to his left so that we were still facing collision. I froze, anticipating the crash of our noggins, but then, in one of those sequences that seems as though it is recorded in slow motion in our brains, I watched as he tweaked his tail and lifted a leg so that his body twisted and he veered past my shoulder with an outstretched wing almost grazing the top of my head.

Once I realized that I had been spared, I could not help being a little philosophical. *Oh, great,* I thought, *wouldn't that have been a way to go out. I can imagine the headlines: "Seminary President Taken to Heaven on the Wings of a Goose."* Yet, though it may seem a bit silly, in a strange way being saved by that little flick of a goose's tail gave me a great deal of peace that day.

The Lord gave me an opportunity to think of his protection in every moment of my life on a day that I was worried about dear friends, the place I serve, and many months of pressure to come. I began to consider the arrangements God had to make for that split-second event of reassurance to happen. What kind of planning did it take for a person, raised in Tennessee almost fifty years ago, and a goose, probably hatched in Canada three years ago, to simultaneously approach a rise in Missouri and come within two feet of one another on the very day that I needed encouragement because of a difficult announcement that I had to make as a result of stock market dynamics that have taken years to develop in a worldwide economy?

The sequence of events that was needed to make all of this converge so precisely is truly mind-boggling. It is beyond all that I could ask or even imagine for God to make a goose's tail twitch at the precise moment needed to fan into flame a flicker of hope in me. In a world that whirls in an endless procession of unpredictable events and personal challenges, we lose track of God's daily acts and his moment-by-moment interventions to preserve us and his purposes for our lives. We know that our God loves us, but amid the pressures of rents to pay, jobs to perform, medical results to await, tests to take, and transitions to make, we wonder still, *Is God able to help me here today?* The Bible's message of a sovereign God who rules over all things in all places among all people and for eternity answers simply to calm our hearts and stimulate our prayers: "He is able."

Praying without doubting God's sovereignty can be tough. Yet those who pray in Jesus' name yield their concerns to his design because they have proof of his care. He is the Good Shepherd who gave his life for his sheep. Now that we know his character, we can trust him with our circumstances. A contemporary song says it well: "The better you know the Shepherd, the easier it is to trust his heart." The reason that we joyfully entrust our lives and our eternities to the Good Shepherd is because he has proven that eternal love fills his heart and will direct our paths.

Key Thought: We offer faithful prayer when we do not doubt that our sovereign God will never forsake his own wisdom and goodness but will powerfully and lovingly answer in the way he knows is best for those who humbly seek his blessing in accord with his will.

Praying without Doubting

Heavenly Father and eternal Shepherd of my
    soul,
for the sake of my dear Savior,
let me live a life of self-doubt and divine trust.
    May I always doubt the sufficiency of my
        wisdom,
        power,
        goodness, and
        faith;

May I always trust the surpassing greatness
of my God's
    wisdom,
    power,
    goodness, and
    faithfulness.
Apply your sovereign will to my finite world:
    Rule as you know is best;
    do as your heart directs;
    heal as you choose.
Forgive me for vision
    willing to see only the reality of this world
        and
    not seizing upon the beauty of the next.
Forgive my sins
    that stand between you and me,
Hide my faults behind the cross
    you stood in their place.
Grant me the zest for life,
    the zeal for righteousness,
    and the comfort for affliction
    that comes when there is no doubt of my
    Father's infinite days,
    limitless ability,
    and unending love.
Send your Holy Spirit to help me
    believe where I lack belief
        and
    supply trust when there seems no cause,
    by reminding me that you sent your Son
    to make me your child
    now and forever.
I commend my soul and my body to you,
In Jesus' name, amen.

4

Praying in the Spirit

Power beyond Our Power

In *The Magician's Nephew*, C. S. Lewis has his lion king, Aslan, send two children, Polly and Digory, on a mission with Fledge, the flying horse. After a while, they discover they have no food. Polly and Digory are dismayed:

> "Well, I do think someone might have arranged our meals," said Digory.
>
> "I'm sure Aslan would have, if you'd asked him," said Fledge.
>
> "Wouldn't he know without being asked?" said Polly.
>
> "I've no doubt he would," said the horse. . . . "But, I've a sort of idea he likes to be asked."[1]

Polly's question may echo our thoughts after reading the last chapter. We may grow concerned that faith in God's sovereignty may also tempt us to reason: Why ask if God already knows? The concern has some merit. If God knows our needs before we ask, then prayer may seem to be wasted effort. In addition, because God knows our needs better than we do, it might seem that we should refrain from praying about anything specific.

Both conclusions would make a good deal of sense, if they did not miss the message in Fledge's astute observation about Aslan: no doubt he knows what to do, but he likes to be asked. God is like that. He knows what we need before we ask (Matt. 6:8), but he still likes to be asked. He urges us to pray in ways that deepen our love and trust of him. Even though we cannot fully understand or anticipate what God should do, we should not hesitate to pray. Not only do our prayers please God, the Holy Spirit uses them to accomplish heaven's purpose on earth.

The Holy Spirit's Part in Prayer

After he reteaches his disciples the Lord's Prayer, Jesus asks them a series of questions: "Which of you fathers, if your son asks for a fish, will give him a snake instead? Or if he asks for an egg, will give him a scorpion? If you then, though you are evil, know how to give good gifts to your children, how much more will your Father in heaven give the Holy Spirit to those who ask him!" (Luke 11:11–13). Jesus again tells the disciples to depend on the fatherly nature of God. If they, being evil (in comparison to the goodness of God), know how to give good gifts to their children, then the disciples should not question that their heavenly Father will "give the *Holy Spirit* to those who ask him." What? Our ears are unprepared for Christ's ultimate promise. We expect Jesus to conclude with the assurance that the heavenly Father will give "good gifts" to his children. The disciples could have expected a little "as your Father knows best" to qualify the promise of good gifts, but who could anticipate the promise of the Holy Spirit—and who would want such a promise?

Our instinctive response to Christ's promise of the Holy Spirit is likely a respectful but slightly disappointed "That's great, Jesus, but . . . uh, err . . . that's not really what I wanted. I really wanted this other thing." When we understand the richness of Jesus' promise, however, we will want nothing other than the promised Holy Spirit.

If we could bottom-line all our prayers, they would essentially be that things in our lives would work out in a way that is best for us. Yes, the string of pearls, the corner office, and the endless vacation would also be nice, but all these are really about the same thing: getting the good life. Sounds impossible, doesn't it? Don't be too sure. There is actually a passage in the Bible that promises "the good life" to those who are committed to God. The apostle Paul writes: "In all things God works for the good of those who love him, who have been called according to his purpose" (Rom. 8:28). This is a fantastic promise! God promises that if we are committed to his purposes, he will work everything together in our life for our good. Most Christians know this promise very well, but few Christians recognize its vital connection to the work of the Holy Spirit through prayer.

Paul introduces God's promise to work all things for our good with a description of the Holy Spirit's part in prayer. If we forget the context, we will miss how special is the heavenly Father's gift of the Holy Spirit to those who pray in Jesus' name. Paul writes:

> The Spirit helps us in our weakness. We do not know what we ought to pray for, but the Spirit himself intercedes for us with groans that words cannot express. And he who searches our hearts knows the mind of the Spirit, because the Spirit intercedes for the saints in accordance with God's will. And we know that in all things God works for the good of those who love him.
>
> Romans 8:26–28

Some claim they know precisely what their prayers should include and what God should do, but even an apostle did not make such a claim. Paul said, "We do not know what we ought to pray for." Still, this lack of knowledge did not stop his prayers, because he understood the ministry of the Holy Spirit.

When we pray, Paul says the Holy Spirit intercedes for us with groans that words cannot express and in accordance with God's will. These two vital ministries of the Holy Spirit make our prayers the most powerful force on earth.

The Holy Spirit's Fervor

When Paul speaks of the Spirit interceding for believers with groans beyond words, he has a type of groaning in mind. This is Paul's third reference to such "groaning" in this passage. First, Paul writes of creation groaning for the fulfillment of God's purpose. The apostle likens these groans to the cries of a mother giving birth (Rom. 8:22). In the next verse the apostle says believers groan with the same pain as they await God's redemption of our bodies—the time when all suffering ceases. Finally, Paul writes that the Spirit also groans, interceding for the Lord's purposes in our lives. With more fervor than we can express, and with the urgency of a mother in childbirth, the Spirit cries before the throne of grace, "Holy God, bless your people. God of Creation, bend the world to your glorious purposes for those seeking you. Heavenly Father, work all things together for your children's good."

The Spirit cries as in the agonies of one birthing new life because new life is being formed—a new world order. The world is hurtling toward the kingdom of God for which Jesus taught us to pray. Yet at the same time, the Holy Spirit groans with urgency and affection beyond our ability to muster, urging the heavenly Father to fashion all things for the good of his children. The Spirit becomes Christ's instrument of intercession for us. He pleads for God to order the temporal world for our eternal good. And because our Triune God cannot deny himself, the Father must respond to the near and dear cries of the Spirit (2 Tim. 2:13). The Father makes all creation bow to our good in response to the pleading of the Spirit.

The realization that the Holy Spirit expresses his fervor through our prayers is as humbling as it is startling. So many times when I pray about difficulties in my church, for struggles of friends and family, or for sin in my heart, there is little urgency in my prayer. I may even fall asleep praying for the salvation of those I love. Too often I am too weak and distracted to pray as I ought. I am like the disciples who fell asleep while Jesus wept (Matt. 26:36–43). My shame can tempt me to give up praying, but the promises of the Spirit strengthen me. My lack of fervor is no reason to rein in my prayers. As I pray so weakly, the Holy Spirit strongly pleads for me with groans deeper than I can express to touch the heart of the Father. And the Father, who sent his Son and his Spirit to be our advocates, loves to listen—and respond.

The entire Godhead exercises all the attributes of the divine nature—each person doing his part—to nurture us. The Holy Spirit kindles the fervor lacking in our prayers so we can be confident that God will accomplish his loving and perfect will for us. But the Spirit does more than provide the needed zeal for our prayers. He also molds the content of our prayers to fit the purposes of God.

The Holy Spirit's Design

The Holy Spirit's fervent intercession is not a swirling hysteria. The Spirit's work is target directed and laser precise. We need this assurance of his careful design because of the limitations of our knowledge when we pray. The Bible says God answers our prayers when we pray in accord with his will, but we struggle to know God's will. So how do we pray according to God's will when we don't know it? God provides the answer by supplying his Spirit. The Holy Spirit intercedes for us in accord with God's will (Rom. 8:26–27).

We know that God's will is to make us more Christlike (1 Thess. 4:3). But apart from this goal, we can rarely (if ever) know God's desires precisely. Were we with Joseph, we would have prayed for his rescue from his brothers' plot to sell him into slavery. Had we been with Mary and Martha, we would have asked God not to let Lazarus die the first time. Were we at the foot of the cross, we would have cried for God to send his angels to the rescue. In each case, the Lord knew better how to accomplish his will for his ultimate purposes.

Our prayers will always be limited by human knowledge and vision. Yet God acts sovereignly. He knows the future we cannot discern and infinite consequences we cannot anticipate. His thoughts and ways are far above ours (Isa. 55:9). We do not have to abandon prayer, however, simply because we cannot fathom the will of God. The Holy Spirit takes our humble prayers and conforms their content to God's will. When we pray in Jesus' name, we offer our desires to God with the foundational desire that he will accomplish his purposes through us. By his Holy Spirit that is exactly what God does, and this is why the Bible urges us to pray in the Spirit (Eph. 3:14–19; 6:18).

When we pray, we never need to pretend that we've got things all figured out. The apostle Paul acknowledged, "We do not know what we ought to pray for" (Rom. 8:26). Even Jesus prayed to his heavenly Father, "Not my will, but yours be done." We risk nothing by confessing our dependence on the wisdom of our God. He already knows our limitations and sent the Holy Spirit to mold our prayers into petitions that please him and satisfy our needs.

I have enjoyed watching a baker decorate a cake with an icing pipe. The icing is globbed into the tube as a yucky, un-formed mess. But that's not the end of the process. Attached to the end of the pipe is a decorator tip. When the baker forces the icing through the tip, the mess gets shaped into intricate designs that make the cake beautiful. The Holy Spirit similarly helps my prayers. I glob my desires into my prayers. I do not intend to make a mess of things, but with my mixed motives and limited vision, I have no assurance that my prayers match God's design. In fact I would hesitate to pray at all if my prayers were God's only direction for accomplishing his purposes. Were my prayers truly capable of binding God's hands, I would be dangerous. My finite, fallible will cannot devise the best course for the universe. Still, I pray because I believe the Holy Spirit works like that decorator tip. He forms my prayers into God's beautiful design for all things.

The Holy Spirit's Wonder

The fervor of the Holy Spirit makes my prayers dear to the Father and the power of the Holy Spirit conforms my prayers to his design. These truths are amazing and comforting. Because the Spirit works through my prayers to do his will, I do not have to know all the answers or emote just the right feeling for God to use me. I do not have to say everything right or do everything right to have all things turn out right. The Spirit takes these burdens from me. The Holy Spirit uses fallible prayers offered in faith to accomplish God's perfect will.

Through the Spirit, God may even use my mistakes to bring about good. This does not mean God wants me to be careless or foolish. I am most blessed when I do everything for God's glory. Yet there are times when I know I have blown it. I fail to accomplish some goal or I say something wrong. My shame makes me crawl toward my God, saying, "O Lord, I am so sorry I let you down." God replies: "Do not despair, child. You were not holding me up. I am the sovereign God who works *all* things for good." Not all *seems* good in this fallen world, and we often lack good motives, but God, through his Spirit, still works all things for his good purposes.

The Holy Spirit ensures that no child of God is useless. Neither age nor infirmity can make insignificant those who seek God's will in the power of the Spirit. He makes our prayers the most potent force in creation. An invalid praying in a nursing home has the ear of heaven. A parent kneeling at a child's bedside has more influence than all the temptations of secular culture. There is no greater ministry than a pastor on his knees in a small church in an obscure town petitioning God for the work of the kingdom. Despite our limited view, Spirit-filled prayer is a force more powerful than the mightiest river, cutting a course through land and time to make all things work together for good.

My family enjoys walking the levee along the Mississippi River near my hometown. My favorite view is near the approach to the power plant. There the river is diverted down a narrow sluice to focus its power on the great turbines that create the city's electricity. The water boils down the channel, developing huge waves and deep sinkholes. Gargantuan whirlpools swirl huge logs and fifty-gallon oil drums as though they were toothpicks and thimbles. The noise rivals the roar of a hundred jet engines.

Despite these displays of raw power, I begin to fathom the potential of the river only when I look beyond the torrent to the town's distant lights. Then I realize the entire city thrives because of the flow of water in these few yards of channel. If so much power resides in this small space, my mind reels considering the power of the Spirit who hovered over the face of the waters at the world's beginning (Gen. 1:2). By the Holy Spirit, God created the oceans of the world, the dry land, the skies, and all that they contain. The power evident in this narrow sluice of the Mississippi River is but a drop in the bucket compared to the world-transforming power of the Holy Spirit. That same Spirit energizes my prayers. He is yet shaping the world around us to conform it to God's will through the prayers of believers.

We have trouble even imagining the implications of God's promises. The Holy Spirit takes the prayers of weak, unwise, fallible humans and transforms them into the pistons of the heavenly engines that drive the material and spiritual universe so that all things work together for good. If God does not answer our prayer for a new red bicycle precisely as we wish, we do not need to worry. He will still use prayer offered in Jesus' name to alter the universe by his Spirit for something better. And if our choices are either a new bike or the Spirit who works all things together for good, then the choice is easy. Any sane person would choose the Spirit, and that is precisely Jesus' promise to those who pray in his name.

The Holy Spirit's Affections

The good the Spirit most desires for us is our transformation into Christ's likeness (Rom. 8:29). He desires for the affections, desires, and ambitions of the Savior to be ours. God knows that when our heart beats in rhythm with his, his greatest joys are ours. We are never richer than when we are emptied of earthly ambitions and fulfilled by Christ's desires. We are never more satisfied than when we are content with his plan for our lives. We know no greater peace than when we are confident his love hedges our lives so that nothing enters except that which makes us more like the Son whom the heavenly Father cherishes. In short, when we have no greater desire than for Jesus to be glorified in us, he grants us the desires of our heart.

New Affections

The Spirit both grants the desires of the faithful heart and stimulates those desires. The world challenges our affection for Christ and his purposes by advertising supposedly superior delights—pleasure, high regard, affluence, and a life without strain. Thus, when we pray in the Spirit, we ask him to stir up within us such affection for God that the affections of the world lose their grasp on our heart and we become more confident that his sovereign will lovingly accomplishes our ultimate good. When the apostle Paul prays for the church at Ephesus, he outlines these priorities of the Spirit's work:

> For this reason I kneel before the Father, from whom his whole family in heaven and on earth derives its name. I pray that out of his glorious riches he may strengthen you with power through his Spirit in your inner being, so that Christ may dwell in your hearts through faith. And I pray that you, being rooted and established in love, may have power, together with all the saints, to grasp how wide and long and high and deep is the love of Christ, and to know this love that surpasses knowledge—that you may be filled to the measure of all the fullness of God.
>
> Ephesians 3:14–19

Paul's prayer culminates with the petition for the Ephesians to be strengthened by the Spirit in their inner being. This power, Paul says, will enable them to grasp how high and long and wide and deep is the love of Christ. And through this love, the Ephesians will be filled with God.

The divine power that fills us comes as the Spirit stimulates a preeminent love for Jesus in our hearts. When we grasp how wide and long and high and deep is his love, our desires are transformed by what the nineteenth-century Scottish preacher Thomas Chalmers called "the expulsive power of a new affection."[2] Through our love for Christ, the Spirit renews and cleanses our desires, creating an appetite for a closer and more mature relationship with God. This new affection overwhelms and drives out previous unhealthy appetites. As a result, our prayers are reoriented.

It is as though, after years of possessing only a black-and-white TV, a generous relative provides us a new high-definition color console. Suddenly the entertainment that appealed to us for so long loses its allure. We desire that which fills our senses with greater sound and color—and seems more real.

Of course, if we wander away from the HD-TV and pass by the room that holds the black-and-white, it may still draw us in and even mesmerize us for a time with its old images. But it no longer has the appeal for us and the power over us that it once did. Our desires have shifted because we have experienced something better.

The believer discovers that life with Christ is better than the empty and colorless pursuit of the world's pleasures. Walking with him, loving him, and loving all that he loves now fulfill us and give our world its color. Old pursuits can still beckon us when we wander from him, but they will never fulfill us as they once did. Our hearts have been forever changed. As a result, the things of the world do not have the power over us that they once had and our prayers reflect more and more the priorities of the One we treasure. We become less selfish, less concerned for personal gain, and more eager to be used for and fulfilled by God's purposes. Jesus' glory becomes the priority of our prayers because we love him above all and most desire that he be honored and pleased. As the prophet Ezekiel beautifully expressed, those in whom the Spirit works become "careful to do" the Lord's will.[3]

Pure Affections

When we are not concerned for the Lord's will, we cannot expect God to answer our prayers. The psalmist writes, "If I had cherished sin in my heart, the Lord would not have listened" (Ps. 66:18). God will never contradict his purposes. He does not answer prayers that feed our selfishness, promote our pride, or undermine what is best for our soul.

If we ask God to make our lives pleasant while at the same time we are pursuing sin, God would damage us by making us comfortable. He will not enable us to ignore his spiritual priorities. Still, God desires to answer our prayers. Out of Fatherly care, he sends his Spirit to convict our heart of sin, reveal the deception of false idols, renew our appreciation of close fellowship with him, and by these measures, purify our affections (John 16:8–11). In short, the Holy Spirit reveals both the misery of our sin and the goodness of our Savior so that our greatest desire is to do his will.

Each spring my family returns to a cabin we love. Months before, we carefully winterized the cabin for the coming cold. Winterizing includes draining the hot water heater so that it will not freeze. In the spring we refill the water heater, and to do it properly, we have to open a valve at the top of the tank. The water filling the heater drives the air out of the tank through the valve. The Holy Spirit similarly fills us with love for Christ to overcome the power of sin. As love for Jesus fills our heart, the air in which our sin and selfishness thrives is forced out. Desire for the things of this world drowns in a heart that is filled up with love for Christ. The Holy Spirit fills our heart with this supreme love for Christ so that his purposes are our greatest desire. Thus Spirit-filled prayer is preeminently Christ-loving prayer.

Changed by God's Spirit

The Holy Spirit turns our prayers inside out, upside down, and backwards. By his work in us, not only do we seek Jesus' priorities above our own, but we actually *want* to seek them. By the Spirit's supernatural work, our natural desires take a backseat and the desires of our Savior take the driver's seat. The Spirit overwhelms us with the depth of Christ's love. Our heart responds with love for him and the desire to serve him, and we most want all that most pleases heaven. Not only does the Spirit use his power to fulfill our prayers in accord with God's will, but he grants us love for Christ that makes us want what God wills.

The Holy Spirit softens hard hearts (see Ezek. 11:19–20; 36:25–27). By impressing us with the wonders of Christ's love, the Spirit changes our priorities, our affections, and our cravings. Through the Spirit, our love for the things of God supersedes our love for the temptations of the world. We grow to understand that the things that attract us materially often attack us spiritually, and we learn to trust that God does not want to deny us any good thing. Praying in the Spirit is not so much seeking magical expressions of God's power to fulfill our desires as it is asking that our Savior's priorities *shape* our desires.

A heart formerly cold toward God does not become warm toward his purposes by a mere act of willpower. While we can will a change in behavior, we do not by an act of will change our estimation of the attractive, appealing, and lovely. I do not suddenly find fudge brownies unappealing simply because I learn their calorie content. My willpower may stop my eating, but it doesn't stop my wanting. But the Spirit can reconstruct the affections of our heart. This is a supernatural work aided by our prayers but not accomplished by them apart from the Spirit.[4]

Many people pray ritualistically for release from destructive urges in the vain expectation that the labor itself will bribe God to unleash his power and eradicate sinful desire. Such persons discipline themselves to pray with the expectation that God will be moved to help them in response to the massive burden of prayer they have assumed to satisfy him. They offer to God that which they don't want to do to get what they want from him. Yet when we pray in the Spirit, we are filled with wanting Christ. We delight to speak to the One whom we love, because we have no greater want than to discover his wants. The discipline of prayer may still challenge us, and our heart may grow cold, but the Spirit-filled heart still yearns for nearness to God and longs for paths back to warm fellowship. We find the path easier when we discover prayer is a privilege for us rather than a bribe for God.

Beloved by God's Spirit

God fills faithful believers with the fullness of his pleasure and power. We have his pleasure, because we pray desiring that his will be done. We have his power, because through such prayers, he chooses to do his will. God does not need our prayers to fulfill his purposes, but—for reasons that are not entirely clear to us—he promotes his glory and our significance by using faithful prayer to advance his kingdom. The Bible says, "The prayer of a righteous man is powerful and effective" (James 5:16).

Much as an old-fashioned steam engine uses coal shoveled into a boiler to power a train, God uses our prayers to empower the engine of divine transformation. Of course he could transform our world without our prayers, just as he could make trains go without natural resources, but he has chosen otherwise. Knowledge of his choices keeps us mining coal and offering prayer.

Praying as Privileged People

Knowledge of how God uses prayer should keep us praying; it should also signal our significance to the heavenly Father. By listening to our prayers, the Father indicates that we are precious to him. By answering our prayers, the Father indicates his willingness to display his glory through us. The Holy Spirit confirms both of these aspects of our privileged position by making our prayers effective.

Through the new affections in our hearts, the Spirit proves to us that we are children of God (Rom. 8:16). Prior to the Spirit granting us confidence in God's provision of our salvation, we hated the things of God (vv. 5–7). Now, however, the Spirit uses our love for Christ and our desire to please him to assure us that we are children of God. No greater evidence of our changed nature exists than the remorse in our hearts when we grieve the Holy Spirit (Eph. 4:30). We still sin, but when we sin—when we succumb temporarily to temptations—we hate it.

The Holy Spirit's grief for sin reflects his concern for the glory of the Father and the Son. Our concern about not grieving the Spirit ultimately reflects our own grief for failing our God. Curiously, this grief is also the Spirit's witness in our heart that we are God's children. Without the Spirit, we might still grieve over the consequences of our sin, but our grief would be for our own hurt. Only the presence of the Spirit in us enables us to love God so much that we truly grieve for the hurt we cause him. In this way godly sorrow for sin confirms—rather than challenges—our standing with God (2 Cor. 7:9–11).

The conviction in our heart that our sin has hurt our heavenly Father assures us of the Spirit's presence. And since the Holy Spirit does not indwell unbelievers, his presence confirms we are God's child. Thus the Spirit's conviction for sin reminds us not only that we still long for God but also that he still loves us. In this way the Spirit uses godly sorrow to encourage prayers of repentance by granting us the confidence that God has not rejected us but still treasures us. Our sorrow for sin confirms the continuing presence of the Spirit of holiness in us.

The Spirit removes our hostility toward God and confirms that God loves us. In this way the Holy Spirit acts as the "seal" of our redemption (2 Cor. 1:21–22; Eph. 1:13; 4:30). The word *seal* reminds us of a signet ring that ancient kings used to mark the validity of their documents. The changes that the Spirit brings to our heart and through our prayers are God's seal validating that we are his. Our new affection for God's purposes as well as our remorse for sin are marks of the Spirit in us. In addition, the Spirit's use of our prayers to promote God's glory confirms how significant we are to the Father.

Praying as Cherished Children

The eternal God listens to mere mortals like us. He grants his Holy Spirit to conform our will to his and to transform our prayers into his purposes. Then he sovereignly exercises his Spirit to work *all things* together for good through our prayers. The Spirit can even use our mistakes to accomplish his good in this world and in our hearts. Love for Christ should keep us from spiritual neglect that leads to mistakes, but the love of Christ overcomes the guilt and effects of our failures. By working beyond all our weaknesses, the Holy Spirit attests how great is the heavenly Father's love for us. The privileges of prayer demonstrate that God treats us as his children, with love as great as he lavishes on his own Son (1 John 3:1).

Even when we do not know the outcome of our prayers, the Spirit's revelation of the heavenly Father's great love encourages us to pray. Some persons will certainly react to a shallow understanding of God's sovereignty with doubts about why we should pray. They reason: *Well, if God is simply going to do whatever he chooses to do, why bother to pray?* While there is some logic in this perspective, such thought contradicts the teaching of the Bible that presents prayer as God's means of fulfilling his purposes. Jesus does not teach us to pray with the precepts of a dumb fatalism—what will be, will be. Instead, he teaches us to offer our desires to God, sends his Holy Spirit to conform our desires to his will, and then promises to empower our prayers by the Spirit so that they accomplish his Father's purposes for us.

We should not have to know the precise ways that God will answer our prayers to be eager to speak to the One who loves us so much—and sovereignly rules all things. Father, Son, and Holy Spirit have promised that faithful prayers will work for our good and God's glory. These assurances make us zealous for prayer no matter how much (or little) we think we know about God's will.

82

As we mature in faith and understanding, our priorities and prayers increasingly grow in harmony with God's purposes so that our prayers also increasingly correspond to God's will. Still, we should never petition heaven without the humility and trust implicit in praying in Jesus' name. By praying in his name, we submit to a wisdom greater than our own to promote a love greater than we can measure.

We do not need to grimace and prepare to guard ourselves when we say, "Okay, God, do your will." Prayer that seeks God's will is not tantamount to receiving a punch in the chops. The Holy Spirit's work assures us that we can offer our desires to God with arms wide open to receive the best that a heavenly Father, who loves us infinitely and eternally, can provide for this life and the next. He who loved us enough to send his Son and his Spirit to us has proven by their ministries that he will respond in ways that are right and loving when we pray.

Key Thought: God does not give finite people the burden of solving the world's problems. Determining precisely how to pray to accomplish God's eternal will would devastate us. Instead, our God provides his Holy Spirit to match the fervor, content, and desires of our prayers to his purposes. The Spirit not only conforms our prayers to God's purposes but in doing so confirms how precious we are to God so that we will seek and trust him more.

Praying in the Spirit

Triune God of all creation,
In the name of Jesus and for his glory,
Send your Holy Spirit to fashion this prayer for
    Christ's praise.

Where my heart lacks seriousness or sincerity,
 supply the Spirit's fervor.
Where my hands lack ability or direction,
 provide the Spirit's power and design.
Where my will lacks resolve or righteousness,
 let the Spirit convict, transform, and
 overrule.
By the Spirit,
 flood my life with the testimony of Jesus,
 to fill my heart
  with love for my true Savior
   and
 to empty my heart
  of love for my false idols.
Immerse me again and again
 in the knowledge of the Spirit's
  power and wisdom
 in the face of my
  weakness and ignorance,
So that I will entrust all matters to you,
 who will work all things
  for my good and
  for Christ's glory.
Hear now the petitions that I offer for the sake
 of my Savior:
(Offer personal petitions here.)

By your Spirit,
 conform these prayers to your will
  and
 by these prayers
 transform my world according to your will.
I pray in Jesus' name, amen.

5

Praying Boldly

As a Child of God

In the classic tale *Cyrano de Bergerac*, a young man named Christian tries to court a beauty named Roxane, but he does not know the words to say. Cyrano, an older man, comes to Christian's aid by standing in the shadows beneath Roxane's window and prompting the suitor with whispered words of lavish prose. The ruse works for a bit, but then the youth bumbles even the words that Cyrano supplies. Cyrano comes to the rescue again and speaks so eloquently for the young man that Roxane's heart yields. Christian and Roxane wed, but Cyrano's words continue to echo with such passion through the story that it becomes clear that they came from his heart. With his own voice and words, Cyrano helped Christian woo Roxane. He wanted the best for her because he loved her too.

Empowered Prayer

The parallels are not exact, of course, but Cyrano's story echoes some dynamics of divine intercession that should make us bold when we pray. Though we may not know the words to say when we pray, another speaks through us for our good. The Holy Spirit does not merely supply the fervor and content of our prayers; he gives us the Savior's voice to make our petitions.

Jesus tells his disciples that when they face persecution for their faith, they should not worry about the words to say, "for it is not you speaking, but the Holy Spirit" (Mark 13:11). This is the same Spirit our Lord says will speak only what he hears from Jesus (John 16:13–15). In short, the Savior promises that the Holy Spirit will provide Jesus' words to his disciples when they stand before persecutors. But the promise of Jesus to speak through faithful followers does not apply only to moments when they stand before persecutors.

The Spirit who speaks only what he hears from Jesus is the same Spirit who groans before the heavenly Father for us when we pray (Rom. 8:26). The implication is wonderful! Through the Spirit we petition the Father with Christ himself speaking for us. The Father answers whatever we ask in Jesus' name because our Savior, God's Son, makes our appeal (John 16:23). We pray, but another prays for us. We approach the heavenly Father, but his Son intercedes. We speak to the King of the universe, but the Prince of heaven speaks on our behalf. Thus we can be very bold, not because we deserve to be heard but because the One who speaks to the Father for us provides us the privileges and power of his identity when we pray.

The Identity of the Son

The apostle Paul tells us that through faith in Christ, God makes us new creatures. Once we were spiritually dead, but now the Holy Spirit gives us spiritual life—regenerating our hearts, reorienting our affections, renewing our wills (Rom. 8:7–14; Eph. 2:1, 4–5). The Spirit transforms us so profoundly that Paul says we no longer live, but Christ lives in us (Gal. 2:20).

Our identity as sinful creatures alienated from the Father has forever been eclipsed by our union with the Son he loves (Eph. 2:13–22). We are now "in Christ" at the same time that he is in us (Rom. 6:1–12). Through this ongoing union, Jesus provides his righteousness for our sin, his strength for our weakness, and his relationship with the Father to replace our alienation (2 Cor. 5:21). Of course, we are the same physical people we always were. We still have the same personalities (though they are being sanctified), and we continue to struggle with weaknesses and fears. But we have a new nature. This new nature possesses spiritual life and is being transformed by Christ's Spirit in us so that we are increasingly Christlike.

In our old nature, we were decaying spiritually—like dead flesh that can only rot away. In our new nature, we are constantly being renewed—like a living body that is always being restored. And because Christ is the One living in us and restoring us, we are becoming more than we were in our old nature. We are becoming more and more like him at the same time that he is giving us eternal life with him. In addition, even before we have Christ's perfection, he shares his identity with us. We too are children of God because Jesus indwells us, sharing with us both his life and holiness. As a result, heaven now receives our prayers on the basis of our having the status of the Father's beloved Son with whom we are united.

The Privileges of Children

Christ's role in our prayers can be compared to the way our judicial system hears cases involving persons who belong to the military. Military personnel are occasionally sued by outside parties for something they did in our nation's service. In such cases, the name of the individual responsible for the problem does not appear on the docket of the case. Rather, the name of the individual's military branch is entered in the record.

The military represents the soldier. As a result, the case is always *Graham Company v. the United States Army* or *Peat Corporation v. the United States Marines* and not *Graham Company v. Private Jones* or *Peat Corporation v. Sergeant Smith.* The individual still must testify, but he speaks to the court with the identity and resources of the branch of the military to which he is united.

When we pray, we speak as the person we are, but the Savior to whom we are united represents us in heaven. The Father hears our prayers, not as the petitions of the fault-ridden persons we are but as the pleas of the infinitely holy and eternally loved Son, our Savior.

Our union with Christ influences every dimension of the Christian life. When we worship, Christ is not only the audience of our songs, but through his Spirit he is also the singer (Eph. 5:18–20). When his servants preach, he is not only the witness of the sermon but the proclaimer (2 Cor. 4:5–7; 5:20; 2 Tim. 4:1–2). When we serve, he is not only the object of our service but the enabler (Phil. 4:13). When we pray, he is not only the Lord whom we seek but the One who speaks.

When we pray in Jesus' name, we pray with his identity. Just as by Christ's intercession we are the ones praying and prayed for, so also in the prayers of believers he is the One being sought and speaking. We speak with the voice of our Savior whenever we pray in his name. As improbable as it may seem, the Father has chosen so to anoint the heart, lips, and tongue of his people that when they pray, the voice of Jesus comes out. The Son speaks for us and through us. This is why the Bible assures us that the Father is attentive to our prayers.

The realization that we pray with the voice of our Savior should make us very bold when we pray. Because Christ intercedes for us, the writer of Hebrews says we can approach the holy, majestic throne of God with confidence of his grace in time of need (Heb. 4:16). We can do away with polite avoidance of matters too difficult to face or too trivial to mention. We do not need to depend on stodgy formulas or arcane speech. We may speak with the familiarity, privileges, rights, and voice of the Son of God whenever we pray to the Father in Jesus' name.

Imposing Prayer

In the parable of the neighbor asking for bread at midnight, which Jesus tells immediately after teaching the Lord's Prayer, he encourages us to pray boldly.

> Suppose one of you has a friend, and he goes to him at midnight and says, "Friend, lend me three loaves of bread, because a friend of mine on a journey has come to me, and I have nothing to set before him."
>
> Then the one inside answers, "Don't bother me. The door is already locked, and my children are with me in bed. I can't get up and give you anything." I tell you, though he will not get up and give him the bread because he is his friend, yet because of the man's boldness he will get up and give him as much as he needs.
>
> So I say to you: Ask and it will be given to you; seek and you will find; knock and the door will be opened to you. For everyone who asks receives; he who seeks finds; and to him who knocks, the door will be opened.
>
> Luke 11:5–10

The request for loaves to feed a guest is more than an imposition; it's downright rude. The hour is midnight! Yet the neighbor knocks anyway. How does he muster such boldness? Christ says the one inside is the seeker's "friend." We will go to our friends with needs that would bother others. We impose, knowing that friends will help us despite our poor planning, foolish errors, or unforeseen circumstances. But God is more than a friend. Jesus reminds us in this passage that our God is our heavenly Father. He listens to us because we speak to him with the voice of his child, and with fathers we can be even bolder than we are with friends.

The first car I ever owned was a Plymouth Cricket, and it helped me understand fathers. The Chrysler Corporation imported the Cricket for only a short time—for good reason. The car was a repair nightmare. I did not realize until I got my next car that people do not expect a car to break down every thousand miles. One of my breakdowns occurred in the middle of the night. I was still hundreds of miles from home but did not panic. I called my father. Though my rescue would rob him of sleep and require hours of his time, I did not hesitate to phone.

I knew that I could impose on my dad because—he is my dad! He is committed to my care. I probably took advantage of my father's care in ways that I am only beginning to understand now that our children are teen drivers. But I am also learning more of what it means to appreciate a child's voice in the middle of the night. I want my children to call me when they are in distress, without being timid or hesitant with me. I want to hear from them because I am anxious to provide the best for them. With these fatherly desires in my own heart, I discover the boldness my heavenly Father wants from me. As I pray in his Son's name and voice, I know he wants to help me.

As I write these words, I am returning from ministry in Africa. While there, I received a call from my son who wanted to tell me his marriage plans. I love knowing that he wants to discuss his life's concerns with me and that distance does not diminish the treasure of our relationship. If I, an imperfect father, so appreciate hearing my child's voice, it helps me understand how my heavenly Father desires infinitely more to hear my prayers offered in the voice of his Son. Jesus makes the point when he asks, "Which of you, if his son asks for bread, will give him a stone? Or if he asks for a fish, will give him a snake? If you, then, though you are evil, know how to give good gifts to your children, how much more will your Father in heaven give good gifts to those who ask him!" (Matt. 7:9–11).

Fathers desire the best for their children. Children who have absolute assurance of their father's care do not hesitate to ask with confidence for anything they need. These simple truths encourage us to bring our heavenly Father concerns that we might be unwilling to take to any other. The matter may be too embarrassing to utter out loud or so painful that we hate even to bring it to mind. Still, the apostle Peter, who knew embarrassment and failure, points us to God and urges, "Cast all your anxiety on him because he cares for you" (1 Peter 5:7).

The Father, who gave his Son for us, has demonstrated his willingness to love us regardless of our faults (Rom. 8:32). We can boldly pray to him.

Pervasive Prayer

Despite the Bible's assurances that God listens to us as a swift-to-forgive and ready-to-help father, we may still be hesitant to pray. We avoid prayers that seem to impose on God, either because we perceive him as harsh or because we perceive him as so good that it seems ungrateful to ask more. Jesus addresses both concerns. He teaches us to pray for matters large and small without fearing that our prayers will offend the Father.

Constantly

The neighbor seeking bread in Jesus' parable does not ask for a culinary masterpiece; he wants only a loaf of bread. The midnight hour makes the request extraordinary. Yet Jesus encourages asking for such a small thing at such an awkward time. The message is clear. Anytime is the right time to pray. Whether the matter is big or little, whether the timing is convenient or pressured, we still have the privilege of praying with the voice of our Savior.

Rev. Frank Barker, former pastor of the large Briarwood Presbyterian Church in Birmingham, Alabama, taught me an important lesson about the privilege of constant prayer. Soon after I became president of Covenant Seminary, I went to Frank to ask for his counsel on leading a large organization. He took me to a cafeteria that was nearly bursting with the lunchtime crowd. We negotiated for a share of a table, and after we had exchanged small talk, I asked Frank for his advice. He started to answer and then stopped himself in midsentence. "This is an important subject," he said. "We had better pray about it before I answer." I have never forgotten that moment.

This man of great stature and experience could have told me whatever came to his mind. I would have listened. Instead, he was more concerned to listen to the Lord. It did not matter that we had already prayed for the meal, that people pressed about us, or that my request for his wisdom was such a small aspect of Frank's ministry. He wanted to make sure the Lord guided all he said and did. This faithful man's devotion was measured not merely by his ability to pray eloquently in the pulpit or by his daily pattern of disciplined prayer but also by his desire constantly to pray.

The willingness to reserve special times for prayer is one mark of devotion. But talking to the heavenly Father all the time is an equally sweet aspect of devotion. It's possible to recognize that all our actions, words, and thoughts are open to God and to rejoice in this constant communion with him through the course of each day (see Ps. 139:1–12). Our entire life can be a continual prayer to God as we direct our thoughts and attitudes to his inspection, honor, and praise. We breathe a word of thanks when the bus arrives on time, fire a mental petition to heaven when facing an upset co-worker, and confess anxiety even as we look into the eyes of a rebellious child. Thoughts can be guarded from sin and cultivated to flower with godly joys by remembering that every reflection of our mind and heart is an offering to God of some praise or petition in the voice of his Son.

Joe Wheeler, in his beautiful tale, "Evensong," introduces the privileges of constant prayer through the diary of a grieving spouse. He writes: "In time much healing has come. And happiness. I've found both in hard work, in getting my mind off of self, and focusing on others instead. God has been good. . . . Has picked up his end of the phone when I've called. For a long time I called him only once in a while; then it was oftener and oftener. Now, we never hang up at all."[1] Virtually every committed and nominal Christian knows to call on God in a time of trouble. But those who truly discover the power of his abiding presence do not reserve prayer for periods of isolated retreat. In addition, they converse with their heavenly Father through private thought on busy streets, in crowded stadiums, in stressed offices, on family outings, and through every day. The great nineteenth-century preacher Charles Spurgeon wrote: "I never pray more than five minutes at a time, but I never go five minutes without praying."[2]

By our union with Christ, our concern for the difficulty of another is an automatic petition for divine aid. Hearts in harmony with the purposes of his glory make their pleasure in God's provision of mountain grandeur or a child's laughter an instinctive prayer of praise. One of the great joys of the Christian life is the privilege of pervasive prayer that allows us constantly to talk to God, knowing that he delights to hear the voice of his child.

There was a time I feared that I had not prayed properly if I had not followed the structure of the A-C-T-S acrostic so many Christians use to guide their prayers. When the order of our prayers follows the adoration-confession-thanksgiving-supplication pattern, we naturally orient our heart and priorities to those of God. Apart from the Lord's Prayer, no other instruction has more aided my understanding of how we should approach God in formal prayer than this ancient method. As early as the third century, the church father Origen taught a variation of this prayer pattern:

> According to our ability, at the beginning of our prayer we must address praises to God through Christ, who is praised together with him in the Holy Spirit . . . and after this, each must place thanksgiving both general—enumerating with thanksgiving God's benefits to the many—and for those things which each has received privately from God: and after thanksgiving, it seems to me that one ought to be a bitter accuser of one's own sins before God, and to ask first for healing so as to be delivered from the state that leads to sin, and secondly for remission of what is past; and after confession . . . we must add petition for the great and heavenly gifts for ourselves, and for people in general, and also for our families and friends; and in addition to all this, our prayer ought to end in praise to God through Christ in the Holy Spirit.[3]

Yet as ancient, excellent, and helpful as this prayer pattern is, it hinders our devotion if it causes us to doubt that we can speak to our heavenly Father as readily, spontaneously, and familiarly as does the Son with whose voice we pray.

Often people ask me to pray for specific needs. I always promise to do so despite my faulty memory and the number of requests. I make the promise because I learned from a mature pastor to send an "arrow prayer" to heaven even as I speak to the person making the request. I cannot model these arrow prayers after the A-C-T-S pattern; they are more the reflexes of my spirit affirming the most basic requests: "Yes, Lord, please help Ginny find her way"; "Watch over John during his surgery"; "Give Marge and Steve your wisdom as they speak to Jerry." My prayers in these moments are not very elegant, but I do not believe God minds. He is more concerned to hear my prayers than to grade their form.

Folding our hands, bowing our heads, and closing our eyes are practices to help us focus and express reverence when we pray. But when the Mack truck is bearing down on our car, we should keep our eyes open, grip the steering wheel, and shout, "Help me, Lord!" He knows what is in our heart and does not require ritual to show that we reverence him and long for his aid.

A young mother I know drove away from a yard sale thinking that her three-year-old was in the backseat of her car. She had left the car for only a few seconds to look at a sale item, but in that time the boy managed to get out of his car seat to pet a dog. Within two blocks she discovered the car seat was empty. She raced back to the yard sale, but her child was not there. Others helped with a frantic search of the neighborhood, but no one found the boy. Too full of worry and fright to think, the mom fell to the ground and could only pray, "Jesus, Jesus, Jesus." The Lord heard and answered the pleadings of her heart, which she did not have words to express. A police car arrived moments later with the child—still clutching the fur of the runaway dog.

The ancient instruction of the church rightly guides the pattern and thought of our devotional and formal prayers. Yet if our prayers are only formal and occasional, we will miss the comfort and blessing of knowing we can pray anytime to the God who is attentive to our cry (see Ps. 34:15). Those who discover that they can constantly speak to their heavenly Father without preamble or pretense will discover the power and joy of the apostle's instruction to "pray continually" (1 Thess. 5:17).

Consistently

We may hesitate to address God constantly in prayer, fearing to bother him with trifles. While in high school I volunteered to help remodel a building for a new church. One day I worked late alongside an older man. We were racing to hammer drywall in place for the seam sealers who were arriving the next morning. At one point he dropped a nail and backed away from the wall to find it. I waited while he circled the floor once and then again looking for the nail.

Finally, I said, "Why don't you get another nail?"

"I just prayed that God would help me find that nail so no one would step on it," he said, "and I feel like I owe it to him to look for it a bit."

"You prayed about finding a nail!?" I asked. "Maybe we ought to save prayer for things a little bit bigger."

"Oh no, Bryan," he said. "The Bible says 'in everything, by prayer and petition, . . . present your requests to God.'"

This man did not know the Greek language of the New Testament or the intricacies of systematic theology, but he understood biblical prayer. Through him I learned that a consistent prayer life brings to God matters both large and small. My friend knew he could bother God with little things because he knew his Father in heaven encourages us to pray about everything.

Small Matters

We may hesitate to approach God because we fear that he is harsh or that we are not appropriately reverent when we "bother" him with minor matters. The response to both concerns should be the same. "Everything" means everything. The apostle means it when he says, "Do not be anxious about anything, but in everything, by prayer and petition, with thanksgiving, present your requests to God" (Phil. 4:6). We can pray about nails as well as about buildings, about minor worries as well as heartaches, and about silly fears as well as tragedy.

The size of the particular issue is not as important as the maintenance of a relationship. I know that if my children turn to me only when the issues are grave, I will rarely hear from them and we will grow distant. I want them to speak to me about small things because such conversation keeps our hearts close. Our heavenly Father has the same concern when he urges us to seek him in everything.

Great Matters

But how bold can we really be? We may pray for nails, but may we also pray for miracles? Again, the answer lies in understanding that "everything" means everything. We may pray about mountains as well as mustard seeds and about cancers as well as colds (see Matt. 17:20–21; John 14:12–14). The Bible never cautions us about the magnitude of our prayers but rather reminds us of the purpose of proper prayer—seeking first Christ's kingdom and his righteousness (Matt. 6:33). When Christ's glory is our aim, nothing is beyond the bounds of our prayer or God's reach. Prayer offered in Jesus' name cannot request too much because the Father desires to glorify his Son as much as possible. Only when we pursue our own glory or pleasure apart from Christ are our prayers limited (James 4:3–10). We may at times struggle to know our own motives, but that's okay; we can pray about this too.

Super prayers are not reserved for super saints. The humblest believer who prays in Jesus' name may appeal to the Father with the voice of the Son. Through our union with Christ, his righteousness rather than ours is the basis of God's favor. When we have the Son's identity and the Father's love, we do not have to worry that only special people can offer "big" prayers. The Scriptures emphasize that everyone who is in Christ prays with his privileges. James writes: "Elijah was a man just like us. He prayed earnestly that it would not rain, and it did not rain on the land for three and a half years. Again he prayed, and the heavens gave rain, and the earth produced its crops" (5:17–18). Sure, Elijah was a powerful prophet, but James's point is that he was a man "just like us" when he prayed so boldly. The Bible urges us to pray about much even if we do not think that we are much.

Miraculous Prayer

The Bible records numerous accounts of God's miraculous deliverance of his people. Big prayers get out of hand not because we request miracles but because we demand them. Even in the Bible, extraordinary acts of providence do not occur every day (see Judg. 6:13; Ps. 74:9). Miracles generally were concentrated at the beginning of eras that inaugurated revelations of God's redemptive plan, and centuries passed with no recorded miracles. Then the Lord used miracles to confirm the authenticity of his prophets' and apostles' ministries or to establish the authority of his Son (for example, see John 20:31; Acts 2:22; 2 Cor. 12:12).

God granted to the church the right to seek miracles as the continuation of Christ's ministry (1 Cor. 12:28). Still, not everyone in the church performed miracles (v. 29). It would be contrary to the pattern of Scripture to expect miracles to continue in large numbers when God is not inaugurating a new epoch of his redemptive plan. Jesus condemns those who demanded signs or miracles as a condition of faith (Matt. 16:4); and the apostles teach that miracles may accompany evildoers as well as the faithful (2 Thess. 2:3, 9; Rev. 13:13–14).

In making these observations about the sequence and purpose of biblical miracles, I do not intend to discourage big prayers. I want only to harmonize our expectations with the Bible's strategy for Christ's glory so that we do not grow anxious about our prayers. In contexts where the gospel is breaking through new cultural or spiritual barriers, the frequency of miracles increases. God remains able to deliver miraculously from difficulty at any time. But if miracles were common, they would not be miracles.

The extraordinary providences, whereby God suspends the physical laws of the universe or marvelously coordinates them, are never designed for entertainment. Rarely do miracles occur for the ease of God's people. In the Bible, miracles come as precursors of the expansion of God's kingdom—often to encourage those who will soon suffer for their faith.

Miracles come in various forms, including divine suspension of natural laws (as when the sun stands still or water turns to wine) or the divine use of natural laws with providential timing (such as finding a fish with a coin or a raven with bread) that provides for our care. We need not be hesitant about praying for either kind of divine intervention. Still, we must trust God to answer as he knows is best. This is why we pray in Jesus' name. By doing so, we always express trust in God's plan as well as faith in his power.

All time and space exist before the face of God. As an expanse of land can be displayed on a map, time and space unfold before our heavenly Father so that he can always see everything at once. He knows the end from the beginning and all that we need before we ask (Matt. 6:8). His unlimited power and wisdom should make us bold enough to ask about matters removed from us in space or time. The Lord promises his people: "Before they call I will answer; while they are still speaking I will hear" (Isa. 65:24). So we may pray for a bus to arrive in the next five minutes and for grandchildren yet unborn to come to faith. I pray even for events that have passed (such as when I have forgotten to pray for my child's exam at the appointed hour) when I do not yet know the outcome. Our time and space do not limit God. Through our prayers we join with missionaries continents away in their battles against Satan and we encourage the faithfulness of our pastors in challenges they have yet to face.

God is infinitely wise and able regarding the sequence of events that will lead to the eternal good of his people. Causes and effects of the magnitude and complexity to boggle the most powerful computer are simple math to God. He controls everything for the *ultimate* good of his people. Thus, despite their prayers, God has kept Christians who were praying for timely airport arrivals from reaching their planes that would later crash. Despite their faithful petitions, the

Lord has denied promotions to believers who were qualified in companies that were later scandalized by the illegalities of their officers.

Most of the time we are unaware of our providential deliverance from daily disasters that would be our lot if we had arrived at the traffic light two seconds earlier or married the person of our dreams or brushed against the sick student we passed in the hall or stepped two inches to the left on a battlefield. But though we do not comprehend the ways God delivers us, they are no less the products of the infinite care of our God and no less the answers to bold prayers for his providential control of all things. The heart of faith believes what the eye cannot observe of God's hand. This is why we continue to pray boldly for his sovereign control of all things to enable us to glorify Christ in all our lives.

Prayer on the Mountain

A few years ago I hiked Colorado's Horn Peak, a mountain with a summit approaching fourteen thousand feet. A friend and I started out on a sunny morning at the end of June. Snow on the mountain from late spring storms made the scenery particularly appealing. About the time we reached the tree line, clouds began to drift over the mountain. Still, the peak was visible, and because I had climbed the mountain several times in previous years, I had no anxiety about the remaining climb.

We reached the peak about noon. Then as we came down the mountain, clouds began to envelop it. Dense fog swallowed us. The landmarks I had used in the past to find my way back were totally obscured. Soon we had trouble even seeing each other more than a few feet apart. The only directions we knew for certain were up and down.

We followed the sound of rushing water for a while, assuming it would lead to a creek we had crossed on our way up the mountain. The rushing water we eventually found in the fog, however, was a waterfall plunging hundreds of feet down a cliff. We traversed the waterfall and tried to get down that side of the mountain, but a glacier bank blocked us. We traversed the opposite direction only to face another glacier bank. So after hours of running into dead ends, we figured out that we had descended halfway down the wrong side of the mountain. There was no safe way to the ground on this side.

By that time moisture in the fog had turned from drizzle to snow. Our lips turned blue, and we worried about hypothermia as we shivered in our summer clothes. We had to get off the mountain, but that required climbing back to the top and descending another face. If we chose the wrong one, we would be led deeper into the mountain range, facing more cliffs and more snow. But there was no option.

Exhausted by the thin air and hours of climbing, we struggled up slippery rock and back to the top of the mountain. The fog was getting thicker. Our landmarks were still hidden, and the cloud layer was stealing our light. An early dusk settled on us.

We hurried as much as we could down another face of the mountain. Yet as we felt our way in the growing dark, we prayed more intensely and began to plan for how we might survive the night on the mountain.

In the camp miles below us, our friends grew aware of our plight. The dense clouds on the mountain and our long overdue return were clear signs of problems. About 5:00 p.m. the camp organized a prayer meeting for us. By 5:30 the clouds had rolled down the mountain and enveloped the camp as well. Jan Roukos, a longtime friend, prayed boldly that the Lord would make time stand still so that we would have enough light to make it home.

On the mountain, darkness was making our descent increasingly difficult. We decided that if we did not find a landmark by 6:00, we would try to construct shelter for the night. The temperature was dropping precipitously and the snow was coming more heavily. Soaked to the skin, we were unsure that we could survive on the mountain, but we were certain we could not descend in the dark.

I glanced at my watch as it approached 5:30. We needed to find a landmark quickly. We increased our pace. Our exhaustion made every minute seem to last forever, but we did not stop. Occasionally I glanced at my watch and rejoiced to see time was creeping by even though our exertions made it seem like more time was passing.

With energy and hope almost gone, we stumbled across a deeply eroded path. I recognized it. The Forest Service had closed this path years ago due to the erosion, but in the near darkness we could not have asked for a better highway. Hours later we reached the camp, exhausted but safe.

As we walked into camp, I glanced at my watch. It was stuck at 5:30. Suddenly I knew why time had crept by when we seemed to be hiking far beyond our stop deadline. I whispered a prayer of thanks for the stopped watch but did not know how thankful to be. Joyful friends soon surrounded us. One laughingly shouted out, "Jan even prayed for time to stand still so that you could get down."

I did not laugh but asked, "When did she make that prayer?"

"About 5:30," was the reply.

I showed Jan my stopped watch and explained what would have happened had it kept running.

Then I shook the watch that had already been shaken violently many times on our stumbling climb, and the second hand started to sweep again. It did not stop until the battery ran out years later. When the watch finally stopped for the second and last time, I mailed it to Jan with a note of thanks for her prayer.

Jan was exceedingly bold in asking the Lord of the universe to stop time. But he is able, and he did so in a most unusual and blessed way. In all honesty, I think that Jan was praying for God to stop the sun the way that he did when Joshua needed more light for battle (Josh. 10:12–14). But in my case, God just stopped my watch. The wonder may not seem as great, but God's timing in staying the tiny movement of a watch mechanism was an extraordinary work of his hand in my life.

As I reflect on all that has happened to me since that scary episode on the mountain, I am increasingly thankful for God's lessons about the value and power of bold prayer. Now I do not fear to impose on my heavenly Father for any of the concerns of my life. Bold prayer about matters both small and great pleases him.

The confidence that we express in such bold prayer is not in the answer we desire but in God. Others have expressed the essence of biblically bold prayer this way: "We should confidently petition God to be God." We do not presume to direct God's will, as if our desires should bind his hands. Our wishes are not his commands. Bold prayer in Jesus' name constantly and consistently takes every matter in our lives to God with the confidence that he is responding by his Spirit as to his own Son's voice with a divine plan and purpose—in his time, in his way, according to his wisdom, with sovereign power, for our Redeemer's glory, and for our eternal good.

Key Thought: When we pray in Jesus' name, we also speak with his voice to the Father. This understanding should make us very bold when we pray. Because we know that we speak to the heavenly Father with the voice of his Son, we should be confident that we can pray consistently about everything in our lives— things great and small, matters that transcend time and space.

Praying Boldly—as a Child

Jesus, Jesus, Jesus.

Note to reader: Remember that our prayers do not have to be long or formal to be acceptable and powerful. God certainly honors thoughtful, reverent prayer, but he also hears the anguish of our heart when we can voice no plea more articulate than calling his name.

6

Praying Expectantly

For All Things Always

On March 9, 1842, the resources of the orphanage run by George Mueller were exhausted. For years Mueller had never asked for money to run the orphanage. He simply prayed for their needs, and God had always supplied. But on this day the money had run out. Mueller's response was to do what he knew best. He gathered friends early in the morning and prayed again. The daily mail provided no relief. Then, just as all hope seemed lost, a special delivery letter arrived. It was a letter that had initially been delivered to the wrong address.

The letter contained a sizable gift mailed from another city. The timely arrival of the misdirected letter meant that the Lord had begun to answer the morning prayer several days earlier. The Lord had interwoven events, thoughts, and timing involving the donor, the postal service, various forms of transportation, bank transfers, and Mueller's prayers to culminate in the needed donation arriving at the crucial moment.[1]

Such events were repeated numerous times in Mueller's ministry. Some reports say such providential rescues of the orphanage occurred hundreds of times. Whatever the precise number, the effect on the ministry is clear. Mueller and his associates grew to expect the Lord's work. Mueller's biographer writes that the minister and those who served with him sang without reservation:

> I believe God answers prayer,
> Answers always, everywhere;
> I may cast my anxious care,
> Burdens I could never bear,
> On the God who heareth prayer.
> Never need my soul despair
> Since He bids me boldly dare
> To the secret place repair,
> There to prove He answers prayer.

What are the marks of expectant prayer, and how may we offer this kind of prayer without presuming on God *and* without abandoning our responsibilities? Again the parable about the neighbor asking for bread at midnight (Luke 11:5–8) gives the answer.

This parable follows the Lord's Prayer and further explains Jesus' instruction to pray for daily bread. The man in the parable must serve an unexpected guest, so he knocks on his friend's door at midnight. Then he spells out his request: three loaves of bread, now. Despite the inconvenience of his request, the man persists until his friend responds. The conclusion Jesus draws: "Ask and it will be given to you."

Jesus clearly teaches us to expect answers to prayers that are specific and persistent. We will address specific prayer in this chapter and persistent prayer in the next.

Specific Expectations

Mueller's biographer says the minister wrote down prayer requests because he believed a permanent record of specific prayers and answers helps accumulate "evidence in our own experience that God is to us personally a prayer-hearing God."[2] In his lifetime Mueller recorded fifty thousand answers to specific prayers. He said that approximately ten thousand of the answers came on the day the prayers were offered. His biographer writes, "On [one] occasion eight specific requests are put on record, together with the solemn conviction that, having asked in conformity with the word and will of God, and in the name of Jesus, he [Mueller] has confidence in Him, that He heareth and that He has the petitions thus asked of Him."

By asking in Jesus' name, Mueller intended not only to ensure Christ's intercession but also to indicate willingness to submit to God's will. Mueller expected God to answer as heaven knew was best. The record of answers to specific prayers also reminded Mueller that God's responses could be more glorious and wiser than the requests he had made. On one occasion Mueller wrote, "I believe *He has heard me*. I believe He will make it *manifest* in His own good time *that He has heard me*; and I have recorded these my petitions this fourteenth day of January, 1838, that when God has answered them He may get, through this, glory to His name."

Mueller's oft-cited expectancy of God's intervention was not a presumptive confidence in God's doing all that the one praying asked. Mueller used Jesus' name with the expectation that God would answer in the way that most glorified the Savior.

Maintaining such expectation must have been difficult after some of Mueller's prayers. During the same time that God was repeatedly rescuing children through the orphanage, Mueller's own child was stillborn, and his wife became grievously ill. Through the course of his life, Mueller buried two stillborn children, a one-year-old son, an adult daughter, and two wives. Why would God allow such vastly different responses to prayer?

Until we are with him, we will not know. But now we can know his divine character, and we can trust the One who provided Jesus for us to listen to us and to do the best for our eternity and his glory.

A Pattern for Worship

Specific prayer is an act of worship demonstrating that we are willing to submit everything in our lives to God—our smallest desires and greatest aspirations. At the same time that we offer specific prayers, however, we complete our worship by submitting our desires and aspirations to God's will in Jesus' name. Praying for specifics opens our lives, moment by moment, to the presence and rule of the Lord. We rivet our attention on him by trusting his hand in every situation. Such constant and specific prayer provides the privileges of a nearly unbroken conversation of the soul with God in a life of perpetual worship.

Specific prayer puts us on intimate terms with our heavenly Father. We trust him to care about the details of our lives, and in doing so, we learn to trust him more. This is why specific prayer does not rule out the need (or desire) to submit our requests to God's will. Jesus prayed specifically and submissively, "Father, . . . take this cup from me; yet not my will, but yours be done" (Luke 22:42). We honor Christ's example when we pray, "Father, please hear and answer this specific request offered out of my desire to seek you in all things. But, Lord, if this request is not all it should be, make it so."

In prayers that are this specific and this submissive, we avoid some common approaches to prayer that call on God without truly honoring him. One unhealthy approach is keeping our prayers so generic and infrequent that we are really only seeking God's blessing on our control of our lives. We courteously recite general prayers for the forgiveness of sins, the good of our nation, and the safekeeping of our family, but there is no pursuit of God (or even consideration of him) for daily specifics. We seem content to ask God to bless *our* management of the details of *our* life. These details, it seems, are best handled by our own grit and wit but, of course, with the hope for God's intercession in times of crisis when he might really be needed.

Modern missionary Rick Gray speaks eloquently of how specific prayer should help direct the heart from self-dependence to true worship:

> I am amazed and saddened, as I survey my life, by how much time I spend trying to find happiness apart from God. You might think that this is an odd confession for a missionary, but it's a true one. So often I have tried to find my security, self-worth and contentment by being "in control" of myself and my situation; or by being "successful" in the things that I do; or by gaining the respect and affection of people; and many other self-styled, man-made schemes. . . . As we were talking over one of the discipleship lessons one day, I was struck by how rarely I involve the Lord in my daily decisions and activities. Of course I spend time alone with Him in the morning but once the day gets under way I act like I'm a one man show with no one to help me. When a problem arises, my first reaction is how can I solve it rather than looking to the Lord for His wisdom and solution. Jesus wants me to lean on Him for everything. Then, and only then, will I begin to find out how truly great, able, sufficient and wonderful He really is.[3]

Specific prayer offered as a continuing act of worship seeks to submit every moment of life to God's wisdom as a means of knowing, loving, and honoring him.

A Pattern from Scripture

Bringing specific petitions to God is not the same as demanding specific responses from God. God commands us to pray specifically for our desires, but our desires cannot command him (Ps. 37:4–5; Phil. 4:6). Those who promise that if we are good enough or pump enough faith into our prayers, we can select the tune God must play, ignore the frailties of their humanity and the faithful saints in the Bible. For example, the apostle Paul performed many miracles during his ministry (Rom. 15:18–19). The apostle also specifically prayed three times that God would remove from him a "thorn in the flesh" (2 Cor. 12:7–9). We do not know for sure the nature of this debilitating affliction, but God did *not* grant Paul's specific request and instead promised sufficient grace to handle the weakness (see chapter 3 also).

The Testimony of Paul

If prayer were a magic wand to remove all difficulty, we would not be able to distinguish prayers for God's glory from desires for our ease. Paul prayed specifically for his healing and urges us to pray similarly. But Paul also prayed with the faith that God would do what was best for him and the ministry of the gospel. Ultimately the apostle's perseverance despite affliction validated his message. Paul's consistent proclamation of eternal promises despite temporal affliction proved that he was not preaching for personal gain or prosperity. All observers recognized that Paul must have really believed his heavenly message, since there was no earthly reward for his efforts. So Paul accepted his affliction and rejoiced that this weakness made his testimony stronger (2 Cor. 12:9).

Prayer provides Christians confidence that God can generate the glory of his Son from the seeds of pain or pleasure. The glory may reflect in earthly rewards or through believers' greater confidence in heavenly promises. If prayer were to bring an end to all hardship, Paul's comments preceding the reference to his "thorn in the flesh" make no sense. The apostle reports he has been imprisoned, flogged, stoned, shipwrecked, sea logged; endangered by bandits, countrymen, and circumstances of all sorts; sleepless, hungry, thirsty, without clothing and shelter, and pressured by church concerns (11:23–28). If specific prayers promised to relieve all difficulty, we might be tempted to say, "Now, Paul, if you just prayed with a little more faith and specificity, life wouldn't be so hard." But the apostle's faith was judged more genuine because it sustained him through hard times (12:9–10). His hardships proved rather than denied his faith.

The Bible supplies multiple examples of faithfulness in the midst of hardship. Paul encouraged his apprentice pastor, Timothy, to drink a little wine for his stomach ailments (1 Tim. 5:23). Why didn't Paul's prayers heal Timothy instead? We could ask the same question when we read that Paul left his companion Trophimus sick at Miletus (2 Tim. 4:20). It seems so obvious to us that God should have answered the prayer of the apostle whom God had used to heal many others (Acts 19:11–12).

Some might assume Paul was lacking in faith at these times of difficulty. We should remember, however, that at the very moment Paul writes these adverse "medical" reports, he writes inspired Scripture. Paul's faith was intact. Should we then assume Timothy's or Trophimus's faith was to blame? No. Paul commends these servants of the gospel. Why then did faithful prayer not heal Timothy and Trophimus? Why did Paul himself struggle with health problems (Gal. 4:13–14)? We do not know the answers. All we know is that Paul and his companions continued to trust God (see 2 Tim. 1:2, 5). Their illnesses were not an automatic sign of inadequate prayer but reminders of how precious was their gospel of eternal life through Christ.

The Testimony of the Faithful

The Bible's "faith chapter"—Hebrews 11—catalogs well-known heroes but then adds to the list the descriptions of unnamed believers who suffered great hardships for their faith. The Bible says these saints were tortured, flogged, imprisoned, stoned, pierced with swords, sawed in two, and made destitute, deprived, and homeless; yet God commends all for their faith (vv. 35–40). Scripture never presumes prayer will remove all suffering. Instead, the biblical writers repeatedly testify that faithfulness through suffering confirms the glory and necessity of Christ's eternal promises.

With specific prayers, Elisha, among the greatest of the ancient prophets, performed miracles, routed armies, healed the sick, and raised the dead. Yet, unlike Elijah, his predecessor, Elisha was not transported from this life on a fiery chariot to heaven. Instead, the Bible simply records that Elisha got sick and died (2 Kings 13:14). So vital was Elisha's godliness that, even after he died, his bones retained healing powers (v. 21). Still, God called him home through illness. We should remember this when through age or infirmity God calls precious servants to their eternal home. We sometimes need to remind other Christians also that a person's present difficulty or death does not allow us to presume the absence of prayer or faith.

A Pattern for Us

Usually the most powerful Christian testimony comes not from the life on "easy street" but from confidence that God's eternal promises more than compensate for this world's heartache. A precious example of faith comes from a man whose daughter died in an accident. She was beautiful, athletic, and a graduate student at a prestigious university. Though she had professed her love for Jesus, her family was not Christian. Her death led them to new life.

After her tragic passing, the young woman's father realized he had nothing in life he valued. "My daughter had become my idol," her father says. "She was the extension of my own ego. Whenever she excelled, I congratulated myself. When she died, I had nothing left of her or myself."

In that emptiness the daughter's words of faith recollected from past conversations and letters began to echo. Eventually the grieving father discovered the profound comfort of heaven's promises. He realized his daughter's passing did not annul his Savior's love, and his failures as a father did not deny the Father's hope. The present separation of parent and child would seem brief in the context of the eternity that would unite them in heaven. And until that time she rested in the love of her heavenly Father. These truths restored hope and life in the earthly father's heart.

The renewed man began to pray that his extended family would find the comfort and joy now giving his life meaning. He prayed specifically for brothers and sisters, nieces and nephews, and his wife. In God's time, each has come to claim Jesus as Savior. The father says that he would not have chosen this path, but the Lord's answers to specific prayers have confirmed God's hand in this family's life and reaffirmed the value to God of the daughter who was taken to him so early. God used a child's tragedy to bring an entire family to himself. Could the eternity of so many have been secured without such soul-shaking pain? Only God knows. Still, this family trusts him, knowing he gave his Child to save a more extended family on earth for eternity.

Great Expectations

The tremendous privilege of approaching the Triune God for specific concerns does not need to be limited to our immediate context. Jesus teaches us to pray for his kingdom to come (Luke 11:2). Our Savior's rule extends far beyond our personal experience but can still be furthered by our prayers. The Bible encourages us to pray for what God alone can change—for church and government leaders, for the salvation of persons in other nations and future generations, for social ills that blight a land and moral decline that endangers the young, for the restraint of Satan and the soon coming of the Savior.

Our failure to pray for such things is usually not due to our lack of concern—they are sometimes our greatest anxieties—but rather due to our limited perspective on the power of prayer. We have the right to speak with the voice of the Son in compelling the armies of the Lord to defeat his enemies, protect his servants, and change hearts in this generation and in the future. When we do not exercise these rights, we indicate we are too willing to depend on human resources or are unable to see that the greatest battles of this world are spiritual. The power we need will be ours only through prayer.

Artillery Prayer

Prayers for specific matters before our eyes should mature into prayers for greater matters that human eyes cannot perceive. We need to understand that the works of believers are rifle shots of God against the enemies of the kingdom, but prayer is the Christian's artillery. Prayer is our most potent weapon for breaking down distant strongholds that oppose the advance of the kingdom of God. For this reason it's been said that prayer is not a seeking after a greater work of God; prayer *is* a greater work of God.

Christian author and leader Os Guinness writes of the artillery work of prayer across generations.[4] He tells of a young mother in 1815 who contemplated taking her life after her husband had perished in a foolish duel. Standing above a river in Scotland, the distraught mother felt the beckoning peace of the dark waters. Then the movement of a plowman working a nearby field caught her eye.

The furrows patterned by the skilled farmer were as artfully etched against the rural landscape as a beautiful painting. Suddenly the world that had become so senseless seemed to have a hint of order, a reason to move on. The young mother reconsidered the needs of her children, the beauty of their love, and the necessity of her life. She moved away from the water.

Months later this same woman came to faith in Jesus Christ. Through a little glimpse of order in this world provided by a plowman, life itself gained purpose. The woman began to plow the fields of the kingdom of God with prayer. She specifically prayed for faith in a dozen generations of her descendants. Os Guinness is one of them.

Through the privilege of specific prayer, the believer applies the power of the Spirit of God through generations, across national boundaries, into the offices of presidents, and into the hearts of thousands. For God to exercise his power in these ways, does he need us? No. But he chooses to work through the prayers of his people to demonstrate his care for us, our value to him, and the significance of our lives in his kingdom. The full power of prayer is beyond mortal comprehension, but the magnitude we can grasp should make us zealous to pray and expectant that God will order our world through our petitions.

Corporate Prayer

When Christians join together in expectant prayer, God's hand often becomes especially evident. A Puritan preacher said, "Individual prayers have the power of each hair on Samson's head, but corporate prayers possess the power of the whole bush."[5] This is *not* because prayers function like the weights on a balancing scale where—if we simply accumulate enough—we can then tip the balance our way. God does not need our numbers to fulfill his purposes. One person praying in God's will is a sufficient majority for heaven's greatest causes. Yet God has designed each of us to contribute to his purposes in different ways (see 1 Corinthians 12). We complete and correct each other with our complementary gifts and talents. The Bible says we function as different members of a body, and together we become the body of Christ (Eph. 4:7–16). We pray corporately "in Jesus' name" with the expectation that his voice will come from this body.

The Bible encourages corporate prayer because when God's people unite their hearts, they are more likely to encourage one another to pray, to examine the appropriateness of their prayer, to maintain their prayer, and to express thanksgiving for God's answers. Charles Spurgeon was asked why so many came to his church in bitter midwinter. He invited his questioner to the basement to see the church's "furnace." The surprise in the basement was no state-of-the-art boiler but rather hundreds of Christians praying for the worship service. Hearts united in prayer warmed each other with God's encouragement even as they promoted his purposes.

The prayer group does not need to be large to receive the promise of God's blessing. Jesus said, "I tell you that if two of you on earth agree about anything you ask for, it will be done for you by my Father in heaven. For where two or three come together in my name, there am I with them" (Matt. 18:19–20). Here again Christ's promise presumes that prayer will be "in my name." The crucial factor for powerful prayer is not the number of persons but the purpose that calls them together.

In August 1806 a Connecticut thunderstorm surprised Samuel Mills and four other college students. Seeking refuge under a haystack, they waited out the storm by praying together. They prayed specifically for the awakening of foreign missions interest among fellow college students. One of the greatest missionary movements in the history of the world followed. Kenneth Scott Latourette, historian of the church's worldwide expansion, says this haystack meeting sparked the great North American missionary movement that continued through the next two centuries.

Great response to specific, corporate prayer still occurs. At the St. Nicholas Church in Leipzig, Germany, strong and weak believers gathered for prayer during the days of Communist domination. The nation had wearied of ineffective political rallies and demonstrations protesting the cruel regime. The prayer group grew weary too. Numbers rose and fell with the mood of the nation. At times only a dozen or fewer prayed in the massive church.

Then in 1989 the Spirit ignited the hearts of his people and hundreds began to come to the church to pray. East German troops blocked the exits of the autobahn on the days of the prayer meeting to keep people from the town. Systematic arrests of the prayer group's leaders were ordered on days prior to the meetings. Communist sympathizers even filled the seats of the church so there would be no place for those wanting to pray.

The praying crowds still came. They stood inside and outside the church while the Communists, at first, listened, and then many joined the prayers. When the numbers of those praying reached the thousands, troops were summoned to handle the anticipated revolt. The people did not revolt but continued to pray with candles in both their hands to show that they had no weapons. Word of the courageous and persistent prayer swept the nation. Though the corporate prayer movement lasted only a few weeks with these numbers, the Communists lost all public support. The government collapsed, and German history began a new chapter without barbed wire, machine guns, and tanks.

A member of the Communist Central Committee later wrote, "We had planned for everything. We were prepared for everything. But not for candles and prayers."[6] What Communists could not prepare for, Christians must do. We pray corporately and specifically because we expect that in his time and according to his purposes, iron curtains will yield and God's Spirit will triumph.

Our Expectations

Knowledge that our heavenly Father loves us, desires to hear from us, and will answer our prayers compels specific prayer with the expectation that great things will come from his hand. As I write these words, the website of the seminary I serve fills with specific requests for those we love. Over the last several weeks we have prayed for a professor's newborn grandson who has been on a ventilator, for a faithful secretary who has been fighting hepatitis, for a graduate in intensive care due to a drug-resistant pneumonia, for another professor's ministry in an influential Muslim nation through highly sensitive and dangerous channels, and for the maturing of ties with a denomination in Ghana that desires our aid. These are the messages on the website today:

- From the professor: Praise the Lord, our grandbaby is off the ventilator! Our daughter-in-law called this AM to tell us that and to say that they are able to hold him in their arms! We praise God for this, and thank you all for your prayers and support to bring him to this point. Please pray that he will continue in this positive direction and will be able to come home soon.

- From the secretary: I am so grateful that I had many, many prayer warriors praying for my health and recovery. I know that God answers prayers. Please continue to lift me up in prayer, that I may continue to recover and that I may regain my strength.
- From the graduate's family: He continues to have a fever. Please pray that this can be controlled. He still has pneumonia in his lungs. Pray that his body will be strong enough to fight this.
- From the Muslim ministry: Enough trust has been established to allow the visits of key persons to discuss their faith in prestigious educational institutions.
- From Ghana: A head of the Ghanaian church will spend a semester on our campus, determining how our resources may help educate leaders for gospel ministry in his nation.

Some of the requests are quite personal; others are of worldwide magnitude. Yet whether the concerns are immediate or long-term, believers have been specific in their requests. They have also asked others to join them corporately in petitioning God. Some answers to these specific prayers have already been revealed; others may not be revealed for many days or years. Some prayers have been answered exactly as we asked; others are being answered in ways we did not expect. Still, all the answers that we have witnessed encourage us to keep praying. Our experience and the testimony of the faithful men and women of Scripture teach us to expect that God will hear us and delight to answer our prayers in the ways he knows are best so that he may be glorified in our heart, across the world, and for generations to come.

Key Thought: Our heavenly Father grants us the privilege of praying specifically for immediate and future matters, privately and corporately, with the expectation that he will hear and delight to answer in the ways he knows are best when his children pray in Jesus' name and with Jesus' identity.

Praying Expectantly

Heavenly Father,

I lift my voice to you in Jesus' name.
I do not ask you to respond because of
    the degree of my goodness or need;
I ask instead that you would hear the voice of
    the One who speaks for me,
    your Son and my Savior.
Because of your infinite love for him,
I know that I can make these specific requests
    and that you will
    listen,
    love,
    and respond.
Please help me with these struggles I face today:
(Offer personal petitions here.)

I know that these are large requests, but I ask
    with the confidence
    that Jesus speaks for me,
    that nothing is impossible with you, and
    that you will answer as is best for me.
Please deal with these matters that make me
    anxious about tomorrow:
(Offer personal petitions here.)

I know that these could be trivial matters for
   One who rules the universe, but I ask
   with the boldness that comes from knowing
   Jesus will speak to you about these matters
   for me, and whatever your Loved One asks
   is not trivial to you.

Lord, I also know that all is open before you.
   Things secret in my heart
   and things secret in the future
   were not hidden from you before I prayed.
I confess my need of your grace to remind me
   that whatever is shielded from human eyes
   is ever before your face.
As Jesus speaks to you on my behalf about these
   matters, please listen to his words with your
   fatherly care and merciful love.
With your divine power, heal my heart, my life,
   and my soul of the effects of these secrets.
Please deal with these matters only you know:
(Offer personal petitions here.)

My Father in heaven, I praise you that I can
   come to you about all these specifics. I
   praise you even more that you let Jesus
   speak for me to you as I pray.
For Christ's sake, hear my prayer and enable me
   to reflect more and more of his character
   and trust in you as I pray.
   All this I ask in Jesus' name. Amen.

7

Praying Persistently

Never, Never Give Up

A modern parable tells of a woman who went to a neighbor's produce stand to purchase grapes. She stood in line while the farmer waited on other customers. Each person seemed to get special attention and the line was long. When the woman finally got to the head of the line, the farmer greeted her with a warm smile of recognition. She ordered her grapes, but the farmer did not immediately fill the order. Instead, he took her produce basket and walked away.

Having to wait again, the woman began to fume, thinking about how the farmer had taken such care of the strangers in front of her, not wanting them to become impatient, but with her he took his time, because he knew his nearby neighbor would be reluctant to put up a fuss. Her smoldering anger was doused, however, by the farmer's explanation as he returned with the basket full of beautiful, perfectly ripened grapes. "I know I kept you waiting," the farmer said, "but I needed the time to get you the very best."

Do Not Lose Heart

Often aspects of patience and waiting are included in Jesus' parables. Apparently we need reminders to persist in prayer when blessings do not seem to come quickly. In the parable of the neighbor asking for bread at midnight, the unprepared host asks his neighbor for bread repeatedly despite the man's explanation that he and his family are already in bed (Luke 11:5–8). In a later parable, a woman receives justice from an unjust judge only after persistent petitions. Jesus concludes that God will be far more willing to "bring about justice for his chosen ones, who cry out to him day and night" (18:7). The Bible says Jesus told this parable to teach his disciples "that they should always pray and not give up" (v. 1).

These parables echo biblical accounts of believers who prayed for months or years before they received answers—and some never saw answers. The prophet Habakkuk begins his prophecy with the question, "How long, O LORD, must I call for help?" (Hab. 1:2). The prophet Daniel, who was delivered from the lions' den, waited forty years for the conversion of the pagan king he served. Sarah miraculously conceived at the age of ninety-nine, but she had waited many years for God to fulfill this promise of a single covenant child. God did not fulfill his promise to make Abraham a father of many nations in his lifetime (and is still fulfilling that promise as he extends the gospel to all nations). Year after year Hannah went to the temple to ask God for a child before God answered her prayer. Naaman, the Syrian, had to dip seven times in the Jordan before his leprosy was removed. The psalmist confesses, "Save me, O God. . . . I am worn out calling for help" (Ps. 69:1, 3). Often those the Bible commends for their great faith did not receive an immediate answer to prayer.

Faithful prayer is not marked by the immediacy of answers as much as by persistent petition. George Mueller, as we have seen, was faithful in prayer. He knew to keep praying when answers were immediate, when answers were delayed, and when answers seemed absent. In his youth, Mueller began praying for the salvation of five friends. He never stopped. One accepted Christ as Savior within two years. Two more confessed their sin and need of Christ's righteousness after ten years. Mueller died with the remaining friends yet unsaved, despite fifty-two years of praying for them. But a few months later, these two placed faith in Christ for eternity as well.[1]

Do Not Fear

Why do we not persist in prayer? We may simply grow weary of asking. We may also grow to doubt that God will answer or has our best interests at heart. Delayed answers to deep hurts can scar faith and can also help feed the conviction that God does not want to answer our petition—at least not in the way that we are asking. Such an attitude is not necessarily wrong. As we will discuss later, one way that we clarify our understanding of God's will is testing it in prayer. Teaching us to yield humbly to God's plan may be his purpose. At the same time, we need to be sure we do not mistake timidity for humility. God is not offended because we return to him. Jesus said, "Do not give up."

Even respect for God's majesty should not make us fretful about approaching his throne with repeated petitions. Our God is not like a city council piqued by repeated requests for a building permit. God is not even offended by this kind of bold persistence:

> I cry to the Lord day and night. I call and call, but he does not seem to listen. I am in deep trouble and need his help badly.

All night long I stay awake lifting up my hands to heaven,
pleading. I think of God and moan, longing for his help. . . .
Has God rejected me? Has his promise failed? Has he slammed
the door in his anger? Sure, I remember the miracles he did
long ago. I can't stop thinking about them. But, O my God,
why have you forsaken me?

These words of persistence and pain seem disrespectful and
even to border on blasphemy. From where do they come? The
Bible! The words paraphrase the psalmist who hurt as we do
and responded to his pain as we may think we cannot (see
Psalms 42 and 77). He expresses to God his true feelings and
repeatedly makes his requests known. If it seems improper
to voice such attitudes in prayer, we should remember that
it makes no sense to hide them. God knows the concerns in
our heart. We might as well be honest.

Do Not Hesitate

Why does God allow such challenging words in Scripture?
He must want to make sure we do not question the rightness
of persistent prayers that strive, even wrestle, to bring heaven
to earth. We do not need to worry that our prayers may become too frequent or repetitive. God commands us to persist
in prayer, and he provides us with accounts of those whose
bold persistence he has blessed. When we pray in Jesus' name,
desiring his purposes and glory, we should not hesitate to pray
again and again. The Father who listens loves his Son, delights
to hear his voice in us, and revels in our spiritual battling for
the glory of his name.

We cannot know the full power of prayer if we neglect or
worry about persistence. Scripture plainly and repeatedly states
that we should pray and pray and pray again. We should not
grow impatient or become discouraged. We should never give
up, fear offending, or hesitate simply because we have already

prayed. Jesus commands repeated petitions. The Bible records them. God honors them.

But why does God want persistent prayer? The question enters every honest heart. Why does the sovereign God, who is able to control all things, who miraculously answers prayer in Scripture, and who tells us that we will receive whatever we ask in Jesus' name, still want persistent prayer? He can answer any prayer in the blink of an eye. Why does he sometimes delay his answer?

God May Do a Better Thing

A couple in our church phoned to ask me to pray about a house they wanted to buy. The house suited the family, was near a preferred school, and was the right price. The couple was closing the deal and wanted no surprises. We prayed over the phone. Later their realtor called. Someone else had offered a higher price.

The realtor's message led to other surprises. More than the deal collapsed. Faith crumbled too. The couple's disappointment watered previously hidden seeds of doubt that God really cared for them. We countered that doubt by praying repeatedly that God would provide the best. Then we waited to see what God would do.

Two weeks later the local building inspector, who was also a friend of the home-searching family, called. In preparation for a loan approval, he had inspected the home they wanted. The house was full of dangerous mold and faulty wiring. The house would require many thousands of dollars to make it safe.

The family that prayed for God to help them buy the house now realized he had done something better. He spared them a financial disaster. They wanted to buy the house, but God wanted to protect them. He had answered better than they had asked.

A home that provided for the family's needs eventually became available. It wasn't pretty on the outside, but the couple no longer doubted God's care. Seeing how God had spared them from greater pain made them confident of his love and the power of prayer.

Persistent prayer in the face of initial disappointment can become the instrument of divine nurture. We grow to trust God more by seeing that often he prepares something better than our initial prayers did (or could) request. In fact God's greatest gifts may come through prayers that seem to be unanswered. Our persistence can help us discover why God blesses by not answering as we ask.

Beyond the Limits of Time

God also uses our persistence to provide blessings that require the passing of time. When we pray for the spiritual maturity of our children or the growth of our church or the effectiveness of an extended medical treatment, we need to return again and again to the throne of grace. Each of these petitions requires God to interweave persons and events in a manner more complex than we can imagine or control. To pray once and then forget about the matter would be both presumptuous and faithless. By persisting in prayer for answers that require the processes of time, we confess to God our perpetual need of him. Regular prayer for continuing needs also testifies to others our confidence in God's continuing work in our lives.

But even if we understand why some prayers take time to answer, how do we handle disappointment with answers that seem to come too late or not at all? When God doesn't seem to answer soon enough, our prayers feel like phone calls to silence. How can we keep from thinking that God doesn't hear or doesn't care? The Bible promises no magic but cautions us to measure God's faithfulness by our understanding of his character rather than by our impressions of our circumstances.

Much about our circumstances will remain hidden until we are in heaven. Jesus has already revealed all we need to know of God's love. Christ's ministry from infancy to the cross took years to fulfill. His people had prayed for centuries for their Messiah. And when he came, some prayed for him to provide immediate political, military, or economic deliverance, but he planned something better. We trust our Savior because he works perfectly, not because he works quickly.

Beyond the Limits of Sight

Jesus has not changed. Just as he provided eternal deliverance through the time of his ministry, he continues to work for our eternal benefit through persistent prayer. As we have already seen, all of space and time exist before the face of our God. He knows the consequence of every action and coordinates all our petitions to fulfill purposes that outlive our prayers and may outlive us. Eric Liddel, the English runner made famous by the movie *Chariots of Fire*, had no idea how God would use his prayer. Out of respect for the Sabbath, Eric refused to run an Olympic race he was favored to win. Eric, who said, "When I run, I feel God's pleasure," then prayed for God to glorify Christ's name as he knew was best. Eric then won Olympic gold in a race he had not trained to run. But that was not the end of the story—or the end of Eric's prayer in Jesus' name.

Eric Liddel's greatest ambition was not winning a gold medal but serving his Savior as a missionary in China. Eric repeatedly prayed that God would use him to bring many in Asia to a saving knowledge of Jesus. After the Olympics, Eric went to China, but his ministry went nowhere. Soon after the young missionary arrived, the Japanese invaded China and placed him in a prison camp, where he died. The apparent waste of Eric Liddell's fame, dedication, and persistent prayers must have discouraged all who knew him and has perplexed believers ever since. But Eric's death was not the end of the story.

The cruelty of the prison camp crushed hope. A camp survivor who later wrote of Eric's life said, "Without the faithful and cheerful support of Eric Liddell, many people would not have been able to manage" the squalor and deprivations of the camp.[2] Though I have seen the story nowhere else, a vivid example of the life-giving support Liddell provided to others in the camp was related years ago by a Covenant Seminary student from Asia. The student said that one day a prisoner edged toward an isolated corner of the camp with a knife hidden in his clothing. He intended to end his misery by taking his life. Eric shadowed the man and eventually spoke. "Look at the birds flying above us," he said, pointing to the barbed wire. "As long as our hearts rest in Jesus, our souls are as free as the birds, regardless of what happens to our bodies." The words revived the hope of the prisoner. He did not take his life but lived to become a training leader for hundreds of ministers and missionaries who have taken Christ's hope throughout Asia.

Another camp biographer wrote of the eventual ministry of the children Eric helped sustain in the prison camp: "Also present were Jim Taylor and Steve Metcalf. Jim Taylor, great-grandson of Hudson Taylor, became General Director of the Overseas Missionary Fellowship, with its more than 900 missionaries. Steve Metcalf went to serve in Japan as an OMF missionary."[3] Eric Liddell's placement in the prison camp at the precise time needed to preserve the lives of generations of key Asian leaders was miraculous—an answer to persistent prayer. We know that Eric's prayer was persistent because others reported that "by the flickering light of a peanut-oil lamp early each morning he (Liddell) and a room-mate in the men's cramped dormitory studied the Bible and talked with God for an hour every day. . . . [His] desire was to know God more deeply, and as a missionary, to make him known more fully."[4] Eric Liddel repeatedly prayed that God would use him to bring many in Asia to a saving knowledge of Jesus. God did.

We cannot know why God chose to work over time in these events. However, we can be confident that the political, social, ethnic, and spiritual developments that God knew would further the gospel were factored into his answer to Eric Liddell's prayer. Eric also assumed such factors would require the passage of time. This is why he persisted in prayer and why we should as well. Before Eric won the Olympic race for which he had not trained, he spoke to the Paris crowds about missing the race he was favored to win. Eric said, "I don't need explanations from God. I simply believe him and accept whatever comes my way."[5] What came his way was both glorious and challenging. It was glorious because Eric's life was used for greater purposes than he could imagine; it was challenging because he would know the full story only in heaven. But we know enough of the story now to strengthen our trust in God's designs and keep praying whatever comes our way.

The movement of the Spirit of God in Asia that rippled from Eric Liddell's life would probably have astounded him as much as it inspires us. In heaven he must rejoice for answers to prayers that persisted through apparent futility. Our challenge is to believe God is yet doing something better than we imagine through our persistent prayer and similar prayers of thousands in decades past, present, and future.

Beyond the Limits of Thought

Our Lord is not limited by our time or our lives as he answers our prayers. The good he accomplishes transcends our vision, our life span, and all realistic expectation. An important example is still unfolding. The early twentieth century marked the first serious efforts of English and American missionaries to reach Muslim peoples. In the first decades of those efforts, mission organizations could count more deaths of missionaries and their children than conversions. However, in the last two decades of the twentieth century and in the first decade of the twenty-first, there have been more conversions of Muslims to Christianity than in all the centuries since Islam began.

Despite the present tensions between the Muslim and Christian worlds, God is doing great things through the faithful prayers and ministries of his people. Of course, many have not lived to see the results of their prayers. But God was, and is, honoring those who persistently pray in the confidence that he will work his perfect will in his timing and according to a divine plan that exceeds our thought.

God Is Doing a Good Thing

But is this fair? While it's easy to concede God is able to do better than we pray, we still wonder why he doesn't answer more readily *when* we pray. He could convert millions in an hour, move mountains in a minute, provide rent money in a second, and heal before we ask. So why does he require persistent prayer? Even if he has better plans than our prayers, it's hard not to ask how God justifies requiring persistence that tests faith and may cost lives.

Creating Christlikeness

To maintain trust, we need to understand the "good" our God wants to accomplish. We persist in prayer presuming that God knits together the fabric of his purposes from the yarn of our prayers, our circumstances, his time, his power, and his knowledge. He works all for a "good" we have previously identified. The apostle Paul says, "In all things God works for the good of those who love him, who have been called according to his purpose" (Rom. 8:28). Then the apostle spells out the "good" God intends from all things: "For those God foreknew, he also predestined to be conformed to the likeness of his Son, that he might be the firstborn among many brothers" (v. 29). Even before we were born, God knew us and was working to make Jesus "the firstborn among many brothers." God does not define our good as the absence of difficulty but rather as our being "conformed to the likeness of his Son." God wants to fill up his eternal family with many siblings of Jesus who are like him. The "good" God most wants for us is our Christlikeness.

Glorifying Christ's Name

When we pray for God to provide good for us, we are implicitly asking to be more like Jesus—for our lives to further Christ's glory. This is another reason we pray in Jesus' name. A prayer in our Savior's name submits more than its content to his purposes. By invoking Jesus' name, we also submit ourselves to Christ's purposes. We ask God to do whatever he wills to make us all that he wants. And we know he wants us to reflect Christ's glory more and more. God alone knows whether Christ will receive more glory through the removal of our trial, through our continued faithfulness in the midst of suffering, or through an ultimate sacrifice that takes us to heaven where pain is replaced by eternal praise of unending joy.

Ultimately we pray in Jesus' name because we *bear* his name. As *Christ*ians, we do not want our prayers or how we respond to God's provision to taint his name. By praying in Jesus' name, we say, "Father, please answer this prayer in a way that helps me glorify my Savior. Conform my prayer to your good purpose for Christ's glory in all the world, including my life."

God's promise to work all things for this good further explains his desire for persistence. Persistent prayer makes us more Christlike by tempering our human selfishness and by strengthening our divine dependence.

Derailing Distractions

If we could snap our fingers and get God to perform on cue, our prayers would promote self-indulgence rather than holiness. An early twentieth-century writer hints at the danger:

> We mostly spend our lives conjugating three verbs: to Want, to Have and to Do. Craving, clutching and fussing. . . . [E]ven on the religious plane, we are kept in perpetual unrest: forgetting that none of these verbs have any ultimate significance, except so far as they are transcended by, and included in, the fundamental verb, to Be, and that Being, not wanting, having and doing, is the essence of the spiritual life.[6]

Prayers too soon answered would merely feed appetites that distract us from God. Were our every wish God's immediate command, Christ's glory would not remain our priority. Christians already struggle to keep Jesus' name our aim. It's hard to imagine how a "get rich quick" mentality could be suppressed by anyone if prayer assured instant, personal gratification.

The key to spiritual happiness is not the Midas touch but trust in God. The fulfillment of the soul is not earthly gain but enjoyment of the Savior. Gain or loss is only an instrument of furthering Christ's glory. Our successes provide opportunities to reflect on God's goodness in the past. Our trials provide opportunities to depend on his sufficiency in the present. Our temporary sufferings teach us to relish his promises for an eternity without tears. Persistent prayer in all circumstances keeps these perspectives fresh and exercises the faith that keeps them strong.

Deepening Dependence

If we never came to the end of our resources, if our children never had to mature, if our churches never faced trials lasting more than a day, and if always our trials vanished with a wish, then we would sense no need to return to God daily and fervently. Yet in such regular communion with him are the spiritual nutrients the soul requires to grow in Christlikeness.

When our children moved through their teen years, my wife and I became increasingly aware of how fine the line was between a prank and a tragedy, between curious exploration and dangerous indulgence, between testing ideas and rejecting faith. We have never prayed harder or more regularly than during this time or felt closer to each other and the Lord in our seeking his wisdom. Only as our hearts became increasingly aware of our limitations and of our dependence on God's provisions did the Christlikeness of our honoring, seeking, and trusting the Lord grow.

Our persistent prayer matured us in ways more profound than we could have anticipated. The good that God provided was not merely his blessing of our children. In addition, praying together nightly for our children deepened our love for each other and for the Lord. This love has become the source of needed strength and great joy in the challenges of our later years.

Concentrating Christ

Prayer that keeps us returning to God day after day cultivates our dependence on him. We learn to trust him and to submit to his timing. These aspects of persistent prayer further the development of Christ's character in us. He petitioned his heavenly Father and regularly depended on him, trusted in him, and submitted to him. When we follow his pattern, we reflect his likeness. But persistent prayer does more than reflect Christ's pattern. By reflecting his likeness, we actually become more of who he is.

The good that God most desires for us, perfecting Christ in us, he furthers by prayer that makes Christ's Spirit more of our ever-present reality and being. Praying persistently in

Christ's name transforms us spiritually. By such prayer the unholy in us becomes more diluted, and Jesus becomes more concentrated. We pray in Jesus' name, in part, because such prayer enables us to approach God in the name of the person whom we increasingly embody.

God Is Doing a New Thing

Understanding that God's primary goal for our prayers is our spiritual transformation helps explain why he may delay his response to some requests. We may want a change in our circumstances, when God wants a change in us. We may need to persist in prayer to discern, for example, that we want a quick solution, but God wants growth in our patience; we want the removal of a troublesome co-worker, but God wants an increase of our love; we want an end to pressures, but God wants us to learn to trust him in everything. William Temple writes, "God is perfect love and perfect wisdom. We do not pray in order to change his will, but in order to bring our will in harmony with his."

Renewing the Heart

The Holy Spirit often uses persistent prayer to enter the busyness of our lives and whisper, "It's time to reconsider. Is this really what God wants? If you have not seen him answer this prayer as you have offered it, then your request or *you* may need to change for this prayer to conform to his will." Because we are so often blind to our own motivations, our frequent return to God in Jesus' name can open our eyes to the changes God wants to make in us to advance our Christlikeness.

Regularly listening to the requests we are making, supposedly for Christ's sake, is a humbling discipline that quickly matures our prayers—and us. John Calvin reminds us that we pray in Jesus' name so "that there may enter our hearts no desire and no wish at all of which we should be ashamed to make him a witness, while we learn to set all our desires before his eyes, and even to pour out our whole hearts."[7] When we carefully examine our prayers to see if they are truly for Christ's glory, his Spirit sensitizes our conscience, reorders our priorities, and transforms our heart. Because God treats us gently, he typically performs each spiritual work in stages and uses our persistence in prayer to serve these purposes.

Restoring the Soul

Discerning the appropriateness of our prayers through persistence is consistent with the instruction implicit in Christ's words. He says, "Ask and it will be given to you; seek and you will find; knock and the door will be opened to you." Modern ears hear these words only as a promise of instantaneous results. But we may just as accurately translate Jesus' words this way: "Be asking and it will be given to you; be seeking and you will find; be knocking and the door will be opened to you." These words that indicate our prayers are to be ongoing and continuous remind us that in praying we often discern what we should pray.

Sometimes we are not sufficiently dependent on God, true to his purposes, or discerning of his will. Our initial petitions may be too limited, immature, or selfish to consider God's intention for our situation or for how he will work in us. In such cases, God uses our persistence to correct us or to help us test what his will is.

We may need correction when we request something that would actually hurt our spiritual development. As children sometimes pray for meals without vegetables, never to get caught, and a good grade despite not studying, adults may pray to be spared the consequences of choices made without God. A businessman may want shelter from years of dishonesty, a spouse may pray to be relieved of all pain in an ill-advised marriage, or a pastor may try to compensate for irresponsibility with the demand that God protect his reputation. In essence each of these prayers is asking God to secure a building that was constructed on a shaky foundation.

God may choose to answer such prayers as they are asked, or he may determine that spiritual priorities are better served by allowing natural consequences. Still, whenever we pray in Jesus' name, God assures us his fatherly heart will control. God will not answer with capriciousness or vengeance those who pray in his Son's name. Jesus came to rescue, not condemn (see Luke 19:10; John 3:17; Rom. 8:1). Persistent prayer in his name will always lead to ultimate blessing regardless of past neglect.

Refining Our Prayer

Persistent prayer also helps us consider whether our aims are in tune with God's will. When prayers seem consistently to remain unanswered, it is not wrong to question whether our petitions align with God's intentions. Determining whether God wants more persistence or a different prayer can be difficult. At times he may want us to keep praying, as did his people for the centuries prior to the coming of the Messiah. Other times God relieves us from a particular burden of prayer by showing that it's not his will at this time. In the next two chapters we will discuss more of how God's will is determined, but for now it is sufficient to know that delayed answers do not necessarily mean that our prayers are wrong, but neither is it wrong to consider altering or refining our prayers.

God may more clearly show us through our persistence that he wants to change our prayer. I once sat by the bedside of an aged mother as her adult children prayed for her life. She had valiantly fought a terrible form of stomach cancer for many months and was now in the final hours of her life. We had prayed for her deliverance from the disease, but her years were advanced and it was not the Lord's will to prolong her life. Yet his hand was on her in these final moments.

The children were not ready to let their beloved parent go and prayed that God would give them more time with her. But her breathing grew more shallow, and finally her breathing and heart stopped.

Then the children prayed again for the Lord to give them more time, and the life monitors around the room lit up with new vital signs. The mother responded to her children's touch and voices. They rejoiced to have her back. Then as the minutes passed, she faded again. The monitors all went quiet. The children prayed again, and again their mother returned to us.

So persistent were the children's prayers that this pattern repeated a half dozen times. The Lord seemed miraculously to respond to these repeated prayers for prolonged life, but the rallies never lasted. Finally, I said to the family, "It seems that it is time to let her go. It appears that the Lord does not want her to stay with us permanently. Let's change our prayer and ask God to take her to the arms of her Savior if that is his will. We know that he is hearing us, and he is assuring us that she will be in glory. We will see her again there. The next time she fades from us, let's pray for the Lord to do as he knows is best for her."

When we prayed in this way, she passed peacefully into glory, but not without the confidence of all in the room that the Lord was present, had heard our prayers, and had beautifully responded to our need. We rejoiced to see his hand so clearly that we knew altering and submitting our prayer to his wisdom would only further his goodness for all.

Uniting Heaven and Earth

Always in biblical prayer a supernatural union occurs between God's wisdom and our need. Some Christians do not understand this fully and define prayer as another kind of merger—the union of our wisdom and God's supply. Such a union could only lead to disaster. We do not have sufficient wisdom to determine what is best for our earthly needs or God's eternal purposes. Were our wisdom responsible for determining the ways that God should supply, we would break under the strain. Therefore God takes this burden from us and promises that he will apply his wisdom to the needs that we faithfully present to him. Persistent prayer helps us both to refine such need according to biblical priorities and to present it to God in the confidence that he will provide the best for those he loves to bless through their prayers in Jesus' name (see earlier discussion in chapters 3 and 4 regarding trust in God's sovereignty and Spirit).

Key Thought: We do not need to be concerned that persistent prayer will offend God or betray a lack of faith. Jesus commends persistent prayer because he works through prayer offered over time to improve our prayers, to further his kingdom, to change us—and to answer.

Praying Persistently

O Father of Jesus in whose name I pray,
I confess that my prayers are too often hasty,
    intermittent, and forgotten.
Keep me coming to you.
Let me remember how great is the love that
    draws me to seek you.
Let me remember how great are my cares that
    drive me to embrace you.

Daily, hourly, and every moment, I need your
    strength and grace and aid.
So let my prayers be
    regular, frequent, and persistent.
Let not your greatness be an excuse for my not
    troubling you with my trifles,
Let not my weakness be the cause for my
    turning from you with my troubles.
The needs I have prayed about before,
    make me willing to express again.
        Sometimes I do not repeat my prayer
            because I fail you.
        Sometimes I do not repeat my prayer
            because I forget my limitations.
        Sometimes I do not repeat my prayer
            because I forsake my loved ones.
Forgive each of these transgressions through
    the mercy of your Son,
    who never fails or forgets or forsakes,
    so that I will keep on praying.
Use my persistence in prayer
    to remind me that you are faithful
        over time,
    to allow me to examine my prayer
        over time,
    to change my prayer, or me,
        over time.
You have never given up on me;
Help me never to give up on you;
And keep me praying, praying, praying,
In Jesus' name, amen.

8

Praying in God's Will

Within the Fence of Righteousness

Several years ago my family spent a year living in the woods. Our cabin lies in a deep forest about an hour outside of town. It is far enough away from my job that I could write undisturbed and near enough to our church that my wife, Kathy, could commute to her job as choir director.

One night after rehearsal, Kathy telephoned. She said she would try to drive back to the cabin despite an impending snowstorm. Only a few flakes had begun sugaring the air, and she expected no problem on the highways. The only possible hitch would be the last leg of the trip—two miles of twisting, gravel lanes through the hills. Those country roads get slippery fast. We decided that I would hike out to the main road to meet her so that we could handle the hills together.

As soon as I began hiking to the main road, I realized we were in trouble. The storm had developed much faster than we had anticipated. Snow was pouring into the lanes like milk filling up a cereal bowl. By the time Kathy arrived, we could not tell there was a road. Kathy looked relieved to see me, but I knew that the real adventure lay ahead.

I got behind the steering wheel, and we began to inch forward, but the drive turned out to be not as treacherous as we had anticipated. We discovered that the fence posts that ran along both sides of the lane still marked our path. As long as we stayed between the fences, we could progress safely, even though we could not see the road in front of us.

Fence posts, like the ones that allowed us to travel safely in a snowstorm, have helped me navigate through one of the most difficult questions about prayer. It's the question about praying according to God's will. Most Christians understand that God answers petitions that we make according to his will. For instance, the Westminster Confession of Faith says, "Prayer is an offering up to God of things agreeable to his will." This historic teaching of the church echoes the plain teaching of the Bible: "This is the confidence we have in approaching God: that if we ask anything according to his will, he hears us. And if we know that he hears us—whatever we ask—we know that we have what we asked of him" (1 John 5:14–15). God promises to grant whatever we ask in prayer that is in agreement with his will. It sounds so simple. The problem is, of course, knowing what God's will is.

How can we know God's will? No question has been asked more often in my three decades of being a pastor and Bible teacher. There's good reason for the question. As we have already seen earlier in this book, even the apostle Paul did not always know God's will. Paul acknowledged, "We do not know what we ought to pray for" (Rom. 8:26).

If even an apostle does not claim always to know God's will, then how can I? Those who claim they can read God like a newspaper seem to have missed the Bible's description of God's inscrutable ways (Eccles. 8:7, 17; Rom. 11:33). A man once told me that his weightlifting son would not lift a bar in practice until he knew God's will about how many times. The desire to please God was commendable, but the presumption that God's will was so easy to read was sad and ultimately destructive to the young man's faith.

Our humanity limits our knowing many specifics of God's will. Still, the Bible teaches us to pray according to his will. How do we do that? The fence posts in the snow help explain.

To pray in accord with God's will, we do not need to pretend to see all the details of the road into the future. Instead, we determine if our prayers are heading in the right direction by steering between two biblical fencerows: the fence of biblical righteousness and the fence of Christian prudence. On this prayer journey we may without shame confess we do not know what to ask for, but if our prayers are kept between these fences, we can be confident that they are within God's will. The remainder of this chapter will deal with praying within the fence of righteousness, and the next chapter will define choices made within the fence of Christian prudence.

Staying within the Fence of Righteousness

Is it righteous? That's the first question when seeking to make a decision or offer a prayer according to God's will. If we want something that is wrong according to God's Word, then praying for it cannot be in God's will. We do not have to wonder if it is God's will for us to steal. It is wrong to steal and wrong to pray to be a successful thief. No amount of fervency or persistence will make God answer such prayer affirmatively. Even asking in Jesus' name will not force God to make someone a better thief. Prayers outside the fence of Christian righteousness are outside the will of God.

Praying for God to bless something wrong, even to accomplish something right, is out of accord with God's will. A businessman who prays for God to bless a dishonest deal so that he can make a larger church contribution is not praying in accord with God's will. A young person only fools himself when he prays that his cheating on an exam will not be discovered so that he can get into a good college, so that he can get a good job, so that he can make lots of money, so that he can support his aging grandmother. If we are praying for something wrong, thinking it will get us to a right destination, we are heading in the wrong direction.

Never does our holy God call us to pray outside the fence of his righteousness. By praying within the fence of righteousness, we honor the authority and standards of the One in whose name we pray. Thus any prayer truly offered in Jesus' name requests only what his Word approves.

Honoring God's Authority

The instructions of Scripture come "by the authority of the Lord Jesus" (1 Thess. 4:2). The path the Bible outlines may feel uncomfortable and may lead to danger, and we may question if there's not an easier way. Still, God's authority, rather than our assessments, determines the proper path. Therefore we should not pray for sexual expression outside of marriage, business success dependent on hiding the truth, national prosperity maintained through injustice, or personal affluence that blinds us to others' needs.

The deep, rural countryside of western Kenya hosts some of the most beautiful landscapes and poorest people of the world. In this remote and impoverished region, Anglican Bishop Simon Oketch serves faithfully the churches of the small Maseno North Diocese. His position would seem unlikely to provide him any distinction, yet he has become a world leader through simple faithfulness to God's Word. At the 1998 Lambeth Conference of the world's Anglican leaders, Bishop Oketch stood to oppose moves by liberal North American and European bishops to approve the ordination of homosexuals.

To the consternation of those who usually dominated such meetings, Asian bishops joined with Bishop Oketch and other African bishops, and ultimately they formed a majority sufficient to approve a statement affirming the Bible's requirement for sexual purity among the church's leaders. Since 1998 Bishop Oketch has been demeaned and even physically attacked for his actions. But his courageous stand has stiffened the resolve of Bible-believing Anglicans throughout Africa and ignited a conviction within them to be the guardians of orthodoxy for seventy million Anglicans worldwide. From the remote jungles and fields of rural Africa, God is exercising his power through a man who put heaven's priorities first. Such heavenly blessing reminds us that there are no people or places remote from God's purposes.

God's Word is more authoritative than personal feelings or priorities. Mess with that order and you will pray outside of God's will. In praying to wed a non-Christian to whom they are romantically drawn, Christians give their feelings greater authority than God's Word. In praying for God to harm someone we refuse to forgive, we vent our anger in a heavenly direction but ignore the directions of God's Word. Praying for a house to sell while keeping buyers unaware of its problems makes our relief more important than our testimony. Our feelings become our authority whenever they determine the priorities of our prayers. In essence we pray in the name of our comfort, our anger, our ambition, or our lust. Imagine how that sounds to God. Praying in Jesus' name requires that we give his Word authority over our desires. We can and must do this in faith that the Good Shepherd will always guide us in the path that is best.

Obeying God's Standards

It is more important to obey God's Word than to try to predict his will. Only through obedience can we know God's will—and pray for it. Consider how little you can predict God's will for you. Does God want you to go to Timbuktu or marry Nancy Sue? Does he want to build faith by healing an illness immediately or to mature faith through a lengthy recuperation? Does he intend to rescue beloved missionaries from danger or use their sacrifice to awaken the church to the need of spreading the gospel?

We can pray with great confidence in God's fatherly care, but we can predict his plans with little certainty. Usually he reveals his will over time through the obedience of his people. As we obey him and pray for his purposes, he perfects his will in and through us. We see his will through the events that unfold, but their significance may not be apparent for years or until we are with the Lord.

Praying for Our Sanctification

Despite our earthly limitations, there remains one kind of petition we know with certainty matches heaven's will. The Bible says, "It is God's will that you should be sanctified" (1 Thess. 4:3). God always wants us to become more like Jesus. We can pray with confidence for the increase of our faith, for the improvement of our obedience, and for the furtherance of our dependence on our Lord. The answer to all of these prayers, of course, requires obedience to God's Word. God does not increase our holiness in any other way. Necessarily, prayers for our sanctification ask God to strengthen our understanding of the requirements given in his Word—and to give us the strength to do them. Prayers in Jesus' name are essentially prayers for God to make us more like Jesus.

Praying to be Christlike is more than pious exercise; it is spiritual power. Prayer in Jesus' name promotes his purposes, and his greatest purpose in our life is for us to reflect him to the world. By praying for God to make us more like Jesus, we ensure that he will do all that his sovereign power determines will most glorify Jesus through us. Heaven and earth bend to his will when we pray for the Father to glorify Jesus in us.

It can be scary to pray that we or our loved ones become more Christlike. A sincere mother once told me that she did not want to pray this for her son because she feared the pain God would have to bring into his life to turn him from sin. Sadly, because the son did not turn from sin, the pain he caused his family crushed them all.

We must remember that we pray to a loving and wise God for our sanctification. While he may choose to prune the wayward branches of our behavior to encourage fresh spiritual growth, he is too wise a spiritual gardener always to prune. He enriches the soil of our lives with blessing, waters our roots with outpourings of love, and bandages our brokenness with his grace. His most frequent answer to prayers for our sanctification is a shower of extraordinary mercy that softens the heart and makes joyful devotion sprout from the driest soul. Even when our sanctification requires God's discipline, his fatherly purpose is only to bring us closer to him. Enfolded in his embrace, we discover greater satisfaction than any sin provides (Heb. 12:11).

Knowing that God's ultimate will is to make us more Christlike takes the pressure off us to figure out precisely how we should pray. We do not need to pray whether it is God's will for us to remain sexually pure, deal honestly in our business practices, or love our spouses. God has already answered these questions. The Christian who wants a sign to confirm that he should be faithful to his wife or act ethically in business or tell the truth to a landlord has already received direction. God addressed these matters in his Word. That sign will not change. Looking for God's will in all the wrong places won't help. We will discover the certain answers to such prayers when we read the Bible and conform our lives to its teaching.

Trusting His Guidance

But what if God's Word does not address the specific concern of our prayer? There are no Bible verses that say take job A or job B, go to church A or church B, or stay with boyfriend A while praying for his maturity rather than moving on to boyfriend B who seems more promising. We often ask God to guide us between alternatives that seem equally righteous. If no options clearly oppose Scripture, how do we determine God's will?

First, do not claim anything you do not know. If God has not addressed the issue in the Bible, do not pretend he has. Only God's standards have moral authority—the right to determine right and wrong. If we label college A as good and college B as evil simply because we have to choose between them, we give ourselves God's status—and commit the sin of blasphemy. We do not have the right to stamp choices as evil or good when the Bible does not. We cannot assume greater authority than God's Word without giving ourselves the status of God.

Christians usurp the Bible's authority when they force varying moral values onto legitimate options the Lord provides. The mistake may occur in a conscientious attempt to obey God. A person may reason, "I do not know what to do. I have these two options, but I can pick only one. Since only one of the options can be God's will, the other must be wrong." Then the person resolves to pray for God to reveal the "right" option with the assumption the wrong alternative will put him outside the will of God. But assigning moral status to matters not condemned or approved in Scripture creates more spiritual problems.

The first problem with labeling right or wrong that which the Bible does not is the creation of choice paralysis. The fear that some choice *might* be wrong leads some people never to make a choice. They date for years without making a commitment, worry about a job option until the opportunity passes, or delay joining a church until children are grown and gone.

The second problem with assigning moral status to legitimate options is ingratitude for multiple blessings. If we saw our choices like apples in a basket, we would not worry that the selection of one of those apples was good and all the other apples were evil. We would simply be glad we had so many apples to choose from. In the same way, it's better to rejoice that God gives the blessing of multiple right choices than to condemn any as evil without the warrant of God's Word.

When we pray for God to guide us among choices that are equally righteous, then we are in essence asking him to give us the wisdom to discern what will most honor him and trusting him with the results (James 1:5). As long as we operate with the wisdom he provides and honor the requirements of his Word, we do not fear operating outside of his will. As long as the matters we are considering are righteous, we can even pray for and choose the most delightful "apples" (i.e., options) he grants. We know that he will so order the events of our lives that, even if we do not immediately see what we think are optimum results, all will work for good because, as our heavenly Father, he will honor and accomplish his will in us (Rom. 8:28–30).

Praying with Humility

Humbly praying for the wisdom to apply God's Word to our circumstances is more important than praying for miraculous signs. While it may seem very spiritual to pray for God to make a flock of birds fly east if his answer is yes and west if the answer is no, Scripture will not endorse such a request. Jesus said, "A wicked and adulterous generation looks for a miraculous sign" (Matt. 16:4). The Bible says that God has already provided sufficient guidance in his Word for our decisions (2 Tim. 3:16–17; 2 Peter 1:3–4). This promise should comfort us. We do not have to wait for mysterious interventions to make good decisions. If we pray for godly wisdom to apply biblical principles, we can make choices with the confidence of having God's approval. Where extraordinary choices must be made, God may provide supernatural guidance, but it's not our prerogative to demand signs.

Praying for signs to determine God's will often results in confusion and creates doubts about God's presence with us. When we demand signs, we are suggesting that God has not given enough guidance in his Word. This means that the instruction of the Bible is not sufficient for our lives and that God has provided inadequate guidance for the millions of Christians to whom he has not revealed miraculous signs through the ages.

Popular Christian culture that encourages Christians to "put out a fleece" to determine God's will compounds our confusion.

In the Old Testament account, Gideon used the sign of dew on a fleece (or its surroundings) to test whether he should obey God's directive (Judges 6). Because he was afraid and doubted that God could do as he promised, Gideon tested God. These are not attitudes or actions for us to mimic. The Lord graciously dealt with Gideon's weakness by providing signs, but the doubting warrior's requests are *not* a model for us. Jesus reminds us that the Bible's standard is "Do not put the Lord your God to the test" (Matt. 4:7). We are not to demand that God perform tricks to prove to us his abilities.

Praying for courage to obey God's Word is a better sign of faithfulness than pretending to know more than God's Word says. Where faithful prayer and biblical thought lead us to believe that competing decisions are equally righteous, we should thank God for the bounty of choices and then choose. Such a choice cannot be wrong when made according to godly principles and priorities. If the choice takes us down a path that God does not want to continue, he is more than capable of redirecting us by future circumstances. Yet God will even use our time on the first path to teach us more about his faithfulness and to conform us more to the image of his Son.

Submitting to God's Righteousness

As discussed earlier, we also pray according to God's will by following Christ's instruction in prayer. To do this, we make our requests for Christ's sake and add, "Yet, Lord, not my will but your will be done." In this way, we submit our petitions to God's will at the same time that we are offering them in Christ's name. In fact praying "in Jesus' name" ensures we are praying according to the priorities of his will and above the priorities of our own.

Submitting to God's will includes continuing to pray faithfully when his answers to our prayers do not meet our expectations or desires. Despite fervent prayer, we may receive rejection letters from colleges or not receive job offers or get the worst of medical reports. When this happens, keep praying. Don't stop! As we have seen earlier, God may answer yes, no, not yet, or beyond all that we ask or even imagine. When it's obvious that God's will is not to answer our prayer as we are offering it, then altering our prayer without doubting his goodness expresses our submission to his lordship and love.

We can always trust that the Good Shepherd has a perfect and loving plan for our lives. When our prayers reach a dead end, the Bible assures us God has a better path. We continue to pray in accord with God's will when we redirect our prayers to asking for his help to walk faithfully in the new path with the confidence that he will never forsake us.

The way we respond to distressing answers to our prayers expresses our humility and trust regarding God's will. As these faith qualities take deep root in our heart, the spiritual fruit that is God's ultimate will for us flourishes. An email sent to comfort a friend struggling with cancer speaks eloquently of this spiritual fruit that is God's highest priority and the Christian's deepest joy:

Dear Susan,

My husband just had his second malignant brain tumor removed last Monday. He has a very aggressive stage four melanoma that has spread to his brain twice in two months. We are truly in God's hands now.

I am writing to lift your family up in prayer as you journey through your illness. You probably have already seen God's plan for you and your family as you face your cancer. He has marked you with a special blessing and standing in his Son Jesus Christ. You are literally illuminating and basking in His Divine Grace at this time.

With our earthly minds, it is difficult to understand the need and place for the type of suffering that goes with this illness. However, you will see and feel with your heavenly hearts that all of God's Glory is being revealed in your lives. You will experience true spiritual oneness with Jesus Christ.

Our Creator has opened a rare window of opportunity for your family to live in total and complete submission to God's will. Most of us take life for granted, encumbered by the trappings and distractions of this planet and never fully enjoy the presence of the Living Savior in our lives. That is about to change for you. A window has been opened for you all to look into heaven, and see God in His Glory and Majesty. Despite your sadness, you will be thrilled by the incredible joy that being selected for his special gift brings. I am there, and I know.

God is hearing your prayers as I write this. He tells us, "I will change your darkness into light and make the rough places smooth; I will not forsake you." Claim these truths as your combat gear to fight this illness.

Through love, prayer, and submission to our Lord, you and your family will find the grace, peace, and strength to carry you through each day. Easy for humans? Of course not. But easy for God? Yes, yes, yes. Give all of your worries and fears to God because He is holding on to all of you right now with all of his might. You are loved by God, Jesus, and the Holy Spirit on earth today and throughout eternity.

In His Love,
A Christian Sister[1]

Responding in faith to all God's answers to prayer grants Christians an understanding of his goodness that transcends the limitations of our bodies and circumstances. Praying for such faith in a time of stress always accords with God's will because he has no greater desire than for our heart to be bound to his with nothing of this world between. And as the letter above so beautifully explains, when nothing in this world is surer or more precious than our trust in God, the brilliance and magnitude of his grace show him to be the treasure we most want and already have.

Resting within the Fence of Righteousness

Responding with faithful prayer to difficult events opens our lives to experiencing the realities of God's grace within the fence of Christian righteousness. Of course, we still have unanswered questions about praying according to God's will. For instance, how do we know when God wants us to continue praying for a matter to bring about his will or to cease praying and bow to his will? How do we know the difference between being hardheaded and being patient or between being submissive and giving up too soon? We know that God may not answer because our desires can be wrong, but it's also possible for our desires to be right and our prayers wrong. How do we know whether to change our desires or to change our prayers? These questions will be addressed in the next chapter as we consider how to follow the path marked by Christian prudence. Still, our first priority when seeking God's will is to pray according to the standards of his Word. Within the fence of righteousness, we are in God's will.

In the summer of 2002, a couple in Birmingham, Alabama, discovered that they were expecting triplets—and that two of the children were conjoined. Friends gathered and prayed, but the news only got worse. The two joined babies shared a heart.

Onlookers encouraged the parents to pray the children would grow apart in the womb or that two hearts would form. In similar situations some Christians feel obliged to say they know it's God's will to heal, as though expressing a wish with confidence will make it happen.

These Christian parents did not pretend to know the Lord's will. They prayed fervently that God would grant health either through a miracle or a doctor. Then they entrusted their hopes and their babies to the heavenly Father, believing he would do what was best. The result was the following note of faith and rest in God from the babies' earthly father:

The news that we received today at the pediatric cardiologist was not as encouraging as we had hoped. The options for separation after birth, as well as the options for survival while still joined, appear to be very low. Even though the details that we are getting from the doctors are much darker than what we wanted, our position has not changed. Before we found out that there was any abnormality at all with this pregnancy, we were walking in dependence upon our Father in heaven to provide for the needs of this new little life. The only thing that has changed in the last week is the number of little lives we are praying for.

We know that God himself has knit these babies together the very way he intended to. We know that he will continue to show himself faithful, no matter what the outcome. It is amazing in some ways to see how God is using these little girls to teach and instruct me. It seems that in their twenty short weeks of life, they have achieved something that I, in my years of being a Christian, have not quite been able to acquire . . . an undivided heart.

Thank you for your continued prayer and concern.[2]

This young father teaches me about praying in God's will. Before and after the babies' difficulties were discovered, their parents prayed for the Lord's care. Clearly such prayer lies within the fence of righteousness. God's Word urges us to pray for our children. Having prayed this righteous prayer, the parents rested in God. They prayed righteously and then walked confidently into the future with the faith that God's answer would be right.

The conjoined twins died soon after birth. Their sister in the womb (the third of the triplets) continues to thrive. God did not will to save the lives of the two babies or to separate them here on earth. But he was not less faithful to them than he was to their sister. God's work is not done. God's sovereign power stretches beyond this world and into the next. There he wills that all his children be made whole and their eternal family will have an undivided heart with them forever. We pray while resting in the promises of a heavenly Father whose will it is to provide this eternal care for all who seek him.

Key Thought: If our prayers involve a choice between alternatives, we should not pray for what the Bible disapproves or label as unrighteous what the Bible does not condemn. We discern God's will by praying for him to provide us with the wisdom and courage to abide by his Word, and then we move forward with the confidence that he will rightly bless prayers offered in Jesus' name.

Praying in God's Will

Dear Lord,
As I come to you in Jesus' name,
Help me also to do his will.
Enable me to understand the commands of
     your Word,
Equip me to obey them, and
Instill in me the resolve to do all that I know
     the Bible
     requires to please and glorify my Savior.

Lead me in the ways that are in accord with
     your will
     by the righteous requirements of
     your Word.
Block me from paths that are contrary to
     your will
     by the hand of your providence.

Help me neither to add nor to subtract from
  the Bible's instruction.
Keep me from crossing any fence that
  your commands have laid.

Guard me from vain requests for signs.
Grant me gratitude for the numerous righteous
  options you can provide.
Guard me from rationalizing prayer
  for wrong things
  with the excuse that they will lead
  to right results.
Grant me strong recollection of your
  instructions in times of stress or decision.

Reveal your commands from the Scriptures
  and then
Let my mind rightly weigh them.
Let my heart rightly desire them.
Let my hands rightly perform them.
Guide me
  by your Word
  for Christ's sake and
  in love and obedience
  in Jesus' name.
  Amen.

9

Praying in God's Wisdom

Within the Fence of Prudence

During my senior year of college, I needed to choose between taking a broadcasting job and entering law school. Neither choice seemed outside the fence of righteousness. While there are scoundrels in both professions, each can be pursued with integrity. I wanted to make the choice that God wanted, so I began to pray that he would reveal his will.

After I had prayed for a while, I began to recognize that I was evaluating my choices solely on how much money and fame I could achieve. As a Christian I did not want to make choices based on worldly priorities. Yet I discovered I was making career choices primarily for selfish reasons. As a result I sought the counsel of a Christian friend to help me think through my motives. He urged me to go to seminary for a year to study Scripture and get my faith priorities back in order.

At first, this seminary suggestion seemed only to complicate my life further—now I had to decide between three choices. I prayed again and asked God to help me understand his will. No revelation came in a dream; none was written on the clouds. Instead, the more I prayed, the more my heart longed for biblical instruction. Ultimately the only proper decision for me was the one not driving me with selfish motives.

This choice was not better because seminary makes a person holier. There was nothing "wrong" with the other choices. I made my choice based on my best judgment that the spiritual priorities God reveals in his Word were not served by jumping on a career track that appealed to my baser motives. I could not point to any Bible verse that says, "Do not go to law school," or "Stay away from journalism." Rather, I discerned God's will by asking his Spirit to bring to my mind the principles of his Word that applied to my situation and then to enable me to use sound judgment about how those principles should affect my decision.

I confess that I went to seminary with a sense of losing ground in my career. Life and my peers seemed to race ahead while I was being left behind in the dust of dozens of ancient theology books. I resolved not to dig in too deeply but to study just enough to prepare me to go to law school the next year. The Lord had other plans. By the end of my first year of seminary, I had been asked to serve as a student pastor of a small, rural church. Against all my expectations, the combination of preaching, teaching, writing, and caring for God's people became my dream job. Everything I loved to do, the pastorate provided.

I never went to law school. Instead, the Lord used the prudential choices that first led me to seminary to take me down another path. On that path I met my wife (she played piano for that little church). The path also led to pastoring historic churches, raising a family that loves the Lord, teaching future pastors, writing books, ministering around the world, and ultimately leading the same seminary I once hesitated to attend.

The choice that seemed least likely to bring earthly reward has been more fulfilling than I ever dreamed.

Probably I made the struggle to discern God's will harder than necessary, because for a time I looked for divine signs to guide me—handwriting on the wall or at least a thunderclap. Such revelations are certainly within God's power, but his regular way of guiding his people is with the priorities of his Word.

My other problem was asking God to guide me between choices before I had evaluated my motives in the light of his Word. As long as I used the priorities of the world to form my options, I remained troubled and confused. No amount of praying about choices that ignore God's Word will bring them into accord with God's will. Prayer will not make an unbiblical choice godly any more than sugar will make liver into candy.

Applying Biblical Principles

Frequently God calls us to apply scriptural principles to choices when there is no obvious right or wrong. Usually we have more uncertainty about these decisions than those where the fence of righteousness clearly marks our path (see chapter 8). Still, we walk a precarious path if we ignore the priorities of the Word. Thus we pray in accord with God's will when we ask him to make us conscious of and submissive to the principles in his Word that apply to our situation. In this way another biblical fence begins to mark our path. The Bible guides us by the fence of Christian prudence. Prudence keeps our prayers and actions within God's will even when choices we must make are not clearly right or wrong.

Only when I asked the Lord to help me weigh the desires of my heart against the principles of his Word did I begin to head in the right direction. And only when I really trusted that honoring his priorities would be the path of blessing did my prayers to do God's will bring his power and peace into my life. I seem to need to relearn this lesson often, and God graciously renews the message. When my prayers are within the fence of Christian prudence, he will bless them. I do not have to see all the details of the road ahead to be assured that prudent prayer will keep me in the path of God's will.

If we are praying for guidance between two seemingly righteous options, the fence of Christian prudence will run alongside the fence of biblical righteousness to keep us within the path of God's will. Christian prudence involves prayerfully seeking wisdom from God's Word, counsel from godly advisors, and insight from the Holy Spirit to make decisions according to the priorities of the Bible. Wisdom from God's Word comes as we are diligent in learning the truths of the Bible through personal reading and church instruction. Counsel from godly advisors comes when we humbly ask mature Christians how they believe God's Word applies to our situation. Insight from the Holy Spirit comes through prayer as we petition the Spirit to help us understand the Bible, the situation, and ourselves so that we can make godly decisions.

Christian prudence never dispenses with issues of right and wrong (the fence of righteousness always stays in place). Rather, prudence enables Christians to apply biblical priorities to decisions for making wise choices among options where none is clearly unrighteous. By prudence, Christians determine options to pursue or petitions to make based on their potential to advance Christ's purposes. The fence of righteousness determines whether our prayer is moral; the fence of prudence helps us determine if our prayer is wise.

Is It Loving?

The first question to consider in weighing the prudence of any prayer is whether our request is loving. Loving prayers consider others' interests above our own (Phil. 2:3–8). Obviously it is wrong to ask God to damage others because of unjustified jealousy or anger, but we must also consider whether sufficient love is behind prayers less obviously unscriptural. There may be nothing at all biblically wrong with praying for a new pony or a new job unless acquiring either one would damage our neighbor or our testimony to him or her. The pony may seem a frivolous and uncaring expense to a community experiencing widespread unemployment. The new job may provide more personal salary but jeopardize our present company's stability and threaten the livelihood of other persons.

The priorities of the Bible will not allow us to consider only ourselves as we weigh the appropriateness of our prayers (1 Thess. 4:9–12). Pastors who must decide when to leave a church for a new position have a particularly heavy responsibility to weigh this decision. I once pastored a church that had just completed a new building program. Shortly afterward, I accepted a call to a more prestigious position. The new position enabled me to use my gifts for Christ's kingdom and required me to do nothing unrighteous, yet I now believe I was wrong to leave the first church. Though the Lord blessed the new work, I think he did so out of his grace and despite my poor care of the church I was leaving.

Doctors take an oath "to do no harm." Ministers should be willing to make the same commitment when deciding God's direction for them. We are not obligated to stay in positions that harm our family or use our gifts poorly, but we should not pray for God to bless choices that disregard the welfare of those whom he has called us to shepherd. All of us, whether ministers or not, are obligated to respect the path God has laid for us and to consider the plans he may have been preparing us to fulfill by giving us experience on that path. Rationalizing selfish decisions with "This is a once-in-a-lifetime opportunity" or "There's no future here" reveals a lack of trust in God's ability to bless faithfulness beyond common expectations.

Always God calls us to put his priorities first and then trust him to take care of the future. The world may not think such decisions wise, but biblical prudence says that it is wise to govern our lives by the priorities of the One who governs the universe. The God who provides a "once-in-a-lifetime opportunity" can provide another at a time that does not damage others. We pray in God's will when we are willing to trust him, forsake worldly wisdom, and be most loving toward others.

Is It Legitimate?

Determining God's will also requires us to assess the legitimacy of our prayer. Legitimate prayers weigh God's interests above our own (1 Cor. 10:31). For example, there is nothing wrong with flipping hamburgers, but persons with teaching or artistic gifts should question if it's legitimate to make fast food their life calling. In this age of affluence, it's possible to rent an apartment, own a car, and afford an entertainment system through jobs that require little responsibility. While there is nothing intrinsically evil about carefree living, Christians should question whether their prayers for a life without challenge are biblically legitimate. Not using our gifts for Christ is as biblically illegitimate as using our gifts only for personal fame, wealth, and power.

The apostle Paul says we should want a quiet life (1 Thess. 4:11). Some commentators say this means our goal should be to have no ambition. This explanation oversimplifies questions we must ask to determine if our prayers are legitimate. The apostle's point is that our prayers should not agitate for our own gain. Paul certainly did not let an ambition for quiet silence his proclamation of Jesus before friends or enemies. Christians should ask: Does my prayer seek Christ's glory? If God were to provide the answer I am requesting, would I be using the gifts and talents God has given me for the advancement of his kingdom? Am I praying for Jesus' name or merely for selfish gain? The world seeks personal peace and affluence. If we pray for nothing more, we should question the legitimacy of our prayers.

Legitimate prayers include requests for things that please us, but only when our greatest joy is the glory of our Savior's name. God may still use the promotion of our name for his glory (Eph. 3:20), yet our prayers are in his will only when the glory of his name is our highest aim. The willingness to be a no-name is a prerequisite of legitimate prayer that requires Jesus' name to have preeminence (Col. 1:18).

Is It Responsible?

God requires us to examine whether our prayer is responsible. Responsible requests pursue our interests according to biblical priorities (Matt. 6:33). This means our requests should not harm our witness for Jesus. The Bible says we should conduct our affairs responsibly so that we will maintain the respect of others and not grow dependent on them (1 Thess. 4:12; 2 Thess. 3:10). These instructions challenge us because they cut across the grain of popular Christian teaching. Regularly we hear accounts of those who leave secure positions and "with a step of faith" depart without a penny for the mission field or seminary or a new ministry. The stories sound very pious, but they are accounts of people who may not be following biblical priorities.

A man who moves his family to the mission field without reasonable prospects of financial support because he "feels called" confuses good intentions with God's will. God requires us to provide for our family's welfare (1 Tim. 5:8). There may be legitimate questions about how God wants the man to fulfill his sense of mission, but there is no question that it's God's will for a family head to be a responsible provider. We should not disregard God's definite will regarding our biblical responsibilities to pursue his possible will regarding our future.

God never calls us to ignore our biblical responsibilities to fulfill his will. People in the Bible who take great risks to honor God's will do not disregard biblical responsibilities of higher priority to do so. Abraham took his family to an unknown land, but he took his flocks and herds with him. The widow who gave her last mite to the Lord did not have the responsibility of a family. Soldiers who leave families to defend their nation fulfill the greater responsibility of protecting many families from enemies.

We must prioritize our biblical responsibilities to discern God's will. He will not require us to go against or shuffle the order of priorities his Word establishes. For example, integrity is more important than success, family security trumps personal desires, and Christian testimony outweighs life itself. The order in each of these couplings is not reversible. We cannot pray according to God's will and prioritize according to ours.

No matter how we try to justify prayers for God to bless irresponsible behavior, we move outside his will when we disregard our biblical responsibilities. Friends of ours tried repeatedly to collect rent from a man who kept saying, "My father will provide the money." Still, the man did not pay his rent. Ultimately he confessed he was praying his heavenly Father would provide the rent even though the man himself was not seeking a job. He was depending on the sacrifice of others rather than using the abilities God had given him to fulfill his obligations.

We should pray for God to use our gifts for Jesus' sake, rather than praying others will serve our interests. We must always listen to our own prayers with an ear as to whether they are designed to make us givers or takers. God loves to answer prayers that enable us to give his joy to his people. But the truest and deepest joys follow prayers that are loving, legitimate, and responsible. Prayers designed only to take his treasures for our gain will not please his heart—or ours ultimately.

There have been times in my life when I confess that my prayers have pushed God for the sake of my pleasure and ambition. Such prayers can still bubble from my weaknesses, but the best and most significant things that God has worked in my life have come when I strove to pray for what was righteous, loving, legitimate, and responsible. Such prayers do not negate petitions for family health, personal success, protection from harm, and just plain fun. I believe God glorifies himself in the happiness of his people who testify that every good gift is from him (James 1:17). I delight to pray for the good in my life that glorifies God. I also pray that he will steer me from prayers that seek my good at the expense of his glory.

An Internal Witness

The question remaining for many reading this chapter is the role of the Holy Spirit. How does he help us determine whether our prayers are in accord with God's will? Is Christian prayer purely a matter of logically connecting the dots of the biblical principles and priorities that apply to our situation? The answer is no. Life is too complicated and the Spirit too wise to make prayer a math of the mind. While we should not depend on external signs, and while we should not ignore the instruction of God's Word, we must remain sensitive to the Spirit's witness in our heart.

Compulsions and Tests

Trying to describe the Spirit's internal witness is like trying to grab the wind, but we have help. Some describe the witness of the Spirit as a "feeling" of being at peace with a decision. Of course, making subjective feelings the foundation of our decisions is dangerous and contrary to Scripture. But to the extent that our feelings are a reflection of the peace that God promises to those who trust and obey him (Luke 2:14; John 14:27), our feelings are not irrelevant in discerning God's direction.

Spiritual peace contrasts with the inner tension or turmoil accompanying prayers not in harmony with God's will (Prov. 25:26; Isa. 57:21). Because the work of the Spirit includes sensitizing our hearts to the requirements of God's Word, we should not dismiss the importance of such feelings of peace (see John 14:26–27). Almost every believer has experienced the work of the Spirit when he makes our conscience particularly aware of some sin or obligation until we address the matter, and then he shifts the spotlight of our conscience to another area of life needing further sanctification.

The ways the Holy Spirit (sometimes patiently and sometimes aggressively) opens the eyes of our heart to life applications of Bible truths remain a mystery of supernatural activity (Eph. 1:17–18). The mystery, however, has certain known features because the Holy Spirit is God. As a member of the Godhead, the Holy Spirit does not instruct us to act in ways contrary to God's Word. God, the Holy Spirit, inspired the Bible's instructions and cannot deny himself (2 Tim. 2:13). He never calls us to do anything that his Word says is unrighteous or not in keeping with its priorities. We may pray about and eventually make choices that are foolish in the eyes of the world, but such paths should be followed only after we examine all options for their adherence to the principles of God's Word.

The Bible tells us to "test the spirits" that seem to compel us by evaluating whether their demands advance the cause of Christ and are consistent with his Word (1 Thess. 5:19–22; 1 John 4:1–2). In other words, we evaluate whether the voice in our heart is that of the Holy Spirit by examining the voice's directives. Do they further the cause of Christ *and* do they further his cause without violating the principles of his kingdom?

The Gas or the Brakes

Our sense of compulsion, as well as our prayer, must be in Jesus' name to comply with God's will. The witness of the Holy Spirit will never take us outside the fences of Christian righteousness or prudence. Rather, the witness of the Spirit functions like a gas pedal and brake on our journey between the fences of God's will. With hearts tuned to the Scripture's priorities by our devotion to Christ as well as our knowledge of his Word, we expect to feel the Spirit's tug and release as we seek God's will. When there is a tug, we press forward with greater vigor within the boundaries of God's Word. When there is release, we hit the brakes without a sense of guilt because we remain within the boundaries of God's Word. We must confess that these tugs and halts are not infallible. They cannot guide us with the same certainty as the fencerows of Christian righteousness and prudence. Still, the promptings of the Holy Spirit are real. Sensitivity to them is necessary to do God's will consistently.

Respected Scottish pastor Eric Alexander gives a modern account of believers praying with spiritual sensitivity.[1] In the 1950s three evangelical ministers—James Philip, George Philip, and William Still—felt compelled by the Holy Spirit to pray that God would revive the Church of Scotland. They met regularly and prayed for an increasing number of Bible-believing pastors. Then, after four years of fervent, joint intercession, the three ministers felt released from this burden of prayer. When they stopped, they confessed to being disappointed. They saw no evidence that God had chosen to revive his church.

Twenty-five years later, these same ministers hosted a conference for Bible-believing ministers who had begun to fill the pastoral ranks. About two hundred pastors came— roughly about one-third of all Scottish ministers. One of the three pastors who had prayed for this increase asked for a show of hands by those who had been converted during those initial four years of prayer. A number in the room raised their hands, including Eric Alexander. Then the conference leader asked those present who had been born during those four years to raise a hand. Most of the rest of the pastors then raised a hand. God had answered the prayer of the original three ministers in a way they could not have expected. Now they also knew why the Holy Spirit had released them from their prayer compulsion after those four years of concentrated effort.

Judging Our Feelings

Praying in accord with God's will should never depend on subjective feelings alone. People can feel contentment or compulsion about many unbiblical and even immoral decisions. Our prayer pattern should first be to ask God's blessing on the things we discern from his Word that are within the fences of biblical righteousness and prudence. For most prayers, these fences clearly mark God's will.

There remain, however, decisions requiring prayer for which no choice is clearly unbiblical. In such cases, we still need to meditate on God's Word and seek Christian counsel. We may also need to pray for God to make his will plain by how events unfold as we yield to special promptings of the Holy Spirit in our heart (John 16:13–14). Such promptings will never lead us outside the fencerows of biblical righteousness or prudence but may grant the holy rest or the holy discomfort that helps us pray according to God's will.

Reading Our Circumstances

Praying in accord with the will of God presumes that we are praying in Jesus' name because we are seeking his purposes. Discerning his purposes does not require secret formulas or mystical visions but rather a growing acquaintance with God's Word that is the expression of his character. Being guided by the Word in our prayers is Christ's primary way of talking with us as we seek his will. The more we immerse ourselves in his Word, the more we are able to walk life's path with Christ at our side, informing our thoughts. Through his Word he points to the flora and fauna of our circumstances as if to say, "I want you to understand this or that." This perspective first underscores the significance of examining all of life in the light of Scripture. Second, this perspective reveals how careful reading of Scripture becomes a form of prayer in which Jesus walks with us to interpret our world.

Through prayer the Holy Spirit orders and generates thoughts in our minds so that we can weigh our circumstances in accord with the priorities of the Word he inspired (1 Cor. 2:4–16; 2 Peter 1:20–21). This process is not simply a function of memory but rather is a supernatural activity by which the Spirit brings to mind those matters most instructive and compelling for the situations we face (Mark 13:11; Luke 12:12). These reflections may come directly from Scripture or may echo from previous experiences and conversations that God has providentially placed along our path (John 14:26). As we live more in harmony with the Savior through our knowledge of his Word and obedience to his Spirit, every circumstance becomes increasingly an instrument of his guidance. The circumstances themselves do not carry the weight of God's Word, but we learn to see their significance in the light of Scripture.

Years ago I was visiting with Covenant College president Frank Brock. As we walked together, he had a quick conversation with one of the college secretaries about the impending marriage of her son. "He still has a year of college left," said the secretary apprehensively. "Yes," said the experienced college leader, "but long engagements can be very hard on Christian young people who want to remain pure before marriage. And if they sacrifice their purity before marriage, they will often struggle spiritually after marriage. If they are definitely on the road to marriage, my advice is to proceed with the wedding and trust God to bless their faithfulness to him."

I have no idea how that conversation stuck in my brain, but I think I know why. Years later my son became engaged to a wonderful Christian during his junior year of college. My wife and I began to pray for God to help us guide our son regarding his plans. Then Dr. Brock's words came back to my memory. Had I not had the experienced leader's wisdom echoing in my mind regarding the importance of protecting the purity of a couple before they are wed, I think I would have let concerns about financial stability and degree completion cause me to object to the timing of the wedding before my son's senior year. Instead, with gratitude in my heart for the Holy Spirit's planting Dr. Brock's words in my mind that helped me carefully consider biblical priorities over worldly pragmatics, we helped our son wed a wonderful woman at the time that was best for them. I recognize that the circumstances of our son cannot be universalized. Others will face factors that would make such an early marriage unwise. My point is only that the Lord provided for us to experience and remember conversations that enabled us to evaluate our circumstances according to his priorities.

Prayer that draws us into quiet communion with God apart from the world enables us to perceive the world with greater clarity. We confess this clarity is counterintuitive. We expect heavenly mindedness to make people naive about the world. Yet prayer that quiets the daily clamor preoccupying our thoughts also opens our soul to the voice of the Savior as he interprets our world by his Word in our heart. The more our heart approaches his in regular, simple, and fervent prayer, the more we resonate with his understanding of the content and contexts of our life. We simply see things as they truly are because we perceive them as does the Creator and Sustainer of all things. Thus we are able to order our prayers and steps more in accordance with his will.

A Global Assurance

But what if we still do not know God's will? We do not need to panic. Remember the position from which we pray. By praying in Jesus' name, we petition God for blessing not on the basis of our discernment but on the basis of Christ's work on our behalf. Prayers offered in Jesus' name are so wrapped in the love, wisdom, and power of God that we remain in his care regardless of the uncertainty of our prayer. Faith in this truth produces profound peace.

As we pray within the boundaries of righteousness and prudence, the God who promises to be our Good Shepherd will direct our paths. If our prayer is a misstep, he will correct it. If our vision is too limited, he will guide us precisely where we should go, because darkness is as light to him (Ps. 139:12). When we pray for the righteous and prudent according to the light of his Word, we can trust God to direct our course (Prov. 3:5–6). Those who so pray in Jesus' name are in his will (and care) on whatever road they take.

To know the comfort that is ours as we pray in Jesus' name, we might imagine again that snowy road mentioned at the beginning of chapter 8. That road symbolizes the route that we must travel to discern God's will about any prayer. Staying between the fences of Christian righteousness and prudence keeps our prayers on the road of God's will. Further comfort comes when we imagine that the icy road is shrunk into a snow globe, such as department stores sell at Christmastime. Should anyone shake such a globe, the snow would swirl and the road ahead would become obscure. In our world, the ground often seems to shake and the way ahead stays unclear. Still, no matter how much snow falls on the road, we should remember that nothing is hidden from our God. This can be our confidence when we pray righteously and prudentially. Even if we cannot see the road ahead, we can rest in the care of the One who can and who holds the whole globe in his hand.

Key Thought: When we pray according to the righteous and prudent priorities of God's Word, we automatically pray according to God's will. If we need additional insight to pray according to God's will, he may provide it by the promptings of the Holy Spirit. Still, even if we do not have full insight into the future will of God, we can have full assurance of his faithful care whenever we pray in Jesus' name.

Praying in God's Wisdom

Dear Lord,
As I come to you in Jesus' name,
Help me also to do his will.
Enable me to understand
 the principles of your Word,
Equip me to weigh your instruction rightly, and
Instill in me the resolve to obey
 all I know the Bible requires
 to please and glorify my Savior.

Lead me in the ways that are
 in accord with your will
 by the priorities of your Word.
Block me from paths that are contrary to
 your will
 by the hand of your providence,
 by the counsel of faithful advisors,
 by the promptings of your Spirit, and
 by circumstances read in the light of
 your Word.

Help me neither to add nor to subtract from the
 Bible's instruction.
Keep me from crossing any fence of Christian
 righteousness or prudence.
Make me sensitive to the Spirit
 so that I pay attention to
  the thoughts he puts in my mind,
  the people he puts in my path,
  the events he puts in my way,

the concern or peace he plants
in my heart.

Forgive me for letting my wants and anxieties
direct me more than
your Word.
Help me discern if I have mistaken my own
compulsions for the Spirit's leading
by making me test every thought against
Scripture's standards.

Grant me faithful counselors
who are committed to helping me
know and do
what the Bible says.
Give me faith that whatever guidance I need
for life and godliness
you provide without ever contradicting
Holy Scripture.

Make your Word
a lamp unto my feet and
a light unto my path,
And give me peace in trusting that the path
you design is right, good, and
more blessed than anything
I could devise.
Guide me for Christ's sake and in Jesus' name.
Amen.

10

Praying Forward

Paddle and Pray

My hometown boasts one of our nation's largest stock brokerage firms. Armed guards secure the entrance and accompany guests through the multibuilding complex. Thousands of employees hustle down sparkling hallways of marble and glass. The boardroom exudes importance, with plush chairs and an imported mahogany table seating forty. Power and wealth seem to ooze out of the walls. Most impressive, however, are the arenas where stock is actually bought and sold.

One salesroom is as large as a football field. Hundreds of people work feverishly behind rows of desks arrayed with thousands of phones, computer keyboards, and video screens. You can almost feel the stocks and securities whizzing by you in the air. Yet despite the millions of dollars moving between portfolios, not one penny is visible. Commerce of great magnitude churns forward without a single dollar bill or coin appearing.

Something similar occurs when we pray. Though we may feel our prayers are simply whizzing through the air without consequence, they are God's means of moving his kingdom forward. When we pray, he applies vast resources of heaven's wealth and power to our world to accomplish Christ's purposes. The fact that we do not see the coinage of our prayers has no bearing on their value or significance. We pray in Jesus' name with the Bible's assurance that our prayers move the kingdom of God forward for Christ's glory. Such assurance should impress us with our privilege of speaking to God and challenge us to consider anything that might hinder or promote the power of our prayers.

More Than a Conversation

Prayer is more than a conversation with God. In biblical prayer, we think God's thoughts after him. The Holy Spirit who indwells us speaks to the Father through the Son with whom we are united, so that God speaks to himself by the thoughts of the believer. These thoughts are ordered by the Spirit. He impresses on our mind principles of Scripture, whispers of the conscience, and impressions from life's experience. These all combine to make our thoughts flow in the furrows that God intends. These furrows are not merely godly patterns of thought but also the soil that God uses to nurture and order the accomplishment of his will. God expresses his power through our prayers! Fellowship with God is prayer's beauty, but we do not grasp prayer's full value until we understand this power.

Too often references to prayer as a conversation with God create a false expectation. Believers think they will speak to God and he will speak back with a voice made audible in our mind or whispered on the wind. Then, for lack of hearing this voice, many consider their prayers ineffective. We could avoid much disappointment by recognizing that the supernatural process of prayer has no easy analogy in our natural experience.

Prayer is not like having a conversation with friends or family. We should not expect our prayers to open a two-way phone line to heaven. Prayer is not so much a dialogue—where we speak and God answers back in words or signs—as a dynamic monologue. In this speaking to God, the Spirit of heaven stirs the spirit of the believer to speak to the heavenly Father. The intercession of the Son carries this prayer to the ear and heart of the Father. Then in deference to the voice of his Son with whom the believer is united, the Father lovingly responds. He causes the thoughts and inclinations of the believer both to engage the divine will (to accomplish God's purposes) and to inform the human will (to desire and perform God's purposes).

When we speak to God, his words in us create the world before us in which he is working. As God once created the living world by the word that he spoke (Ps. 33:9; John 1:1–3), he now re-creates the world in which we live by speaking his words through us (1 John 2:14; Rev. 19:13–16). We become co-creators of this new world order by virtue of the Word of God in us that by his Spirit is working all things together for our good (Rom. 8:28, 32). As the Spirit makes our words the word of Christ before the Father, our prayers re-create all things by changing the world before our eyes *and* by changing how the eyes of our heart perceive the world (Eph. 1:18–23). Our world is remade by prayer that both changes our world and changes us. The result is the same: prayer changes our world.

Mystery remains for our human minds regarding how God blends the material and spiritual, as well as the human and the divine, to accomplish his purposes through finite creatures such as we. But we should not let our inability to explain fully his ways deny us a grasp of the beauty and hope of the new reality that will pour through our prayers. Even glimpses of the power and glory that God promises as consequences of our prayers will transform our world.

When I was an adolescent, my eyesight began to deteriorate quite rapidly. The medical advice of the time was to fit me with hard contact lenses that would not only enable me to see better but also progressively reshape the contour of my eyes. The lenses changed my world in two ways. First, they physically changed me. The features of my eyes were reformed. Second, and more important, the lenses changed my world by enabling me to see that which was previously denied to me because of my poor eyesight. My life changed dramatically. Class work that had previously been too difficult for me became accessible because I could see the teacher's writing on the board. Sports suddenly became fun because I could see the ball. I went from feeling muddled, confused, and lost every day to believing that I could deal with whatever came because I could now see my world as it really was.

Prayer works similarly. By our prayers not only does God physically change the material universe for us, he changes us so that we can perceive the world and eternity as they really are. Everything becomes new through our prayer.

Prayer never disappoints when we understand that God intends for our petitions not only to change the realities we see but also to enable us to perceive his greater realities. As we pray God's thoughts, his divine activity and eternal assurances become more substantive and accessible to us. The way God makes his reality our own challenges our heart and mind. Still, the process of praying his thoughts should not be considered so saintly as to be reserved for the spiritual elite.

God renews his image in all believers. Though his image in us has been marred by our sin nature, God is constantly transforming us into the likeness of Christ by the Spirit. As our thoughts, attitudes, and actions are increasingly controlled by the Word and by our union with Christ, our inclinations conform more and more to the will of God. Our prayers align with God's desires, because that which grieves him grieves us and that which pleases him pleases us. Increasingly we think and act more in accordance with his will and thus increasingly interact with our world (and everyone in it) through prayers that reflect God in us. And since God forms our world in response to our prayers that are his desire, our prayers increasingly form the world according to his will.

More Than a Monologue

Prayer blesses us, not so much because God promises to speak in response but because God promises to listen. We do not speak into a void when we pray. Our words are not whistling in the wind; they direct arrows of concern to the heart of our heavenly Father, who applies infinite love, wisdom, and power to bend creation to serve us. The certainty that this God listens—really listens—provides comfort, strength, and hope even when God seems silent.

The experience of Hannah, the prophet Samuel's mother, reveals the significance of a listening God. She had grieved for years because she could not bear children. Out of the crucible of her pain, she cried out to God. She addressed him as "Lord Almighty" or, literally, the Lord of Hosts (1 Sam. 1:11). And thus calling to the God who commands the armies of heaven, she pled for a baby. She actually expected the King of the universe to listen to her. Such prayer may seem very presumptuous, but it is the privilege of every Christian.

We expect the Lord of all creation and eternity to listen to us when we pray because he promises he will. When our disappointment is great and our fears are large, he says we can cast all our cares on him because he cares for us (1 Peter 5:7).

Healing thrives in the recognition that God listens. Christian psychiatrist and author Paul Tournier says, "It is impossible to overemphasize the immense need that humans have to be really listened to, to be taken seriously, to be understood."[1]

When no one really listens, trying to understand our pain, we feel utterly alone, despairing, and without purpose. Yet even if our afflictions do not evaporate, when we find a confidant who cares, we are strengthened and emboldened in the face of our adversity. By lending us his ear, God shares with us his strength.

I rediscovered the power of the divine ear during my freshman year in college. Far from home, without close friends, and not able to make the grades I wanted, I felt alone and futureless. I walked the rocky shore of Lake Michigan with the sense that my life was as precarious as my footing. Everything dear to me was gone. I collapsed in despair only to have the words of a long-forgotten Sunday school teacher echo in my mind: "Tell it to God. He listens." No lightning bolts or thunderclaps interrupted my tears. No mysterious apparition spoke. Yet I rose from the ground with new hope. My grades were still a struggle, my loved ones were still distant, but I had told it all to God and he had listened. That was enough.

God's listening is enough simply because we need to be heard. A six-year-old girl recently wandered away from grandparents and spent two days in Arkansas wilderness. She conquered her fears and survived her experience by befriending a caterpillar in the cave where she slept.[2] The caterpillar met some deep need for companionship we all share, but such an ear provides no real aid. In contrast, God's listening strengthens us through the confidence that the One who controls the universe loves us, understands our concerns, and will provide the best response.

This provision may come immediately—as when God granted Hannah a child—or it may be delayed—as when God delivered later generations through Hannah's child. Still, we have the assurance that the One who listens to us is our Father, and he holds our world in his hands. We glimpsed the peace our Father's care provides when a friend's son lost money collected from his newspaper route. The child had no resources to cover the loss. He went to his father in tears.

The father simply said, "I will take care of it." The boy's tears evaporated. The problem wasn't yet fixed, but it had been put in the hands of the one who could handle it and who promised his care. That was enough.

When we pray, God listens to our heart *and* he changes our world. It's difficult to say which is the greater blessing. Each response is astounding in itself, and together they point toward prayer benefits more vast than we can comprehend. Yet an inkling of the privileges that are ours fills us with power, peace, and fresh desire to pray.

Power Hindrances

The answers God gives to our prayers astound *and* challenge us. We are astounded to think that God actually forms our world by his word as he listens to our prayers. We are challenged by this truth to approach our prayers with greater expectation and to guard our prayers from anything that would hinder their effectiveness. The Bible says that attitudes and activities that damage our fellowship with God have the potential of limiting our prayers.

Sin

Since our prayers are the means by which God expresses his will through us, sin, which is counter to his purposes, will hinder our prayers. The Bible identifies the following specific causes of weakened prayer:

1. *Personal disobedience.* "If anyone turns a deaf ear to the law, even his prayers are detestable" (Prov. 28:9).
2. *Unconfessed sin.* "If I had cherished sin in my heart, the Lord would not have listened" (Ps. 66:18).
3. *Unforgiving attitudes.* "And when you stand praying, if you hold anything against anyone, forgive him, so that

your Father in heaven may forgive you your sins" (Mark 11:25).

4. *Uncaring actions.* "If a man shuts his ears to the cry of the poor, he too will cry out and not be answered" (Prov. 21:13).

5. *Selfishness.* "When you ask, you do not receive, because you ask with wrong motives, that you may spend what you get on your pleasures" (James 4:3).

6. *Self-promotion.* "And when you pray, do not be like the hypocrites, for they love to pray standing in the synagogues and on the street corners to be seen by men. I tell you the truth, they have received their reward in full. But when you pray, go into your room, close the door and pray to your Father, who is unseen. Then your Father, who sees what is done in secret, will reward you" (Matt. 6:5–6).

7. *Family discord.* "Husbands, in the same way be considerate as you live with your wives, and treat them with respect as the weaker partner and as heirs with you of the gracious gift of life, so that nothing will hinder your prayers" (1 Peter 3:7).

8. *Failure to pray.* "You do not have, because you do not ask God" (James 4:2).

9. *Doubt.* "If any of you lacks wisdom, he should ask God, who gives generously to all without finding fault, and it will be given to him. But when he asks, he must believe and not doubt, because he who doubts is like a wave of the sea, blown and tossed by the wind. That man should not think he will receive anything from the Lord" (James 1:5–7).

10. *Community/national disobedience.* "Both the house of Israel and the house of Judah have broken the covenant I made with their forefathers. Therefore this is what the LORD says: 'I will bring on them a disaster they cannot escape. Although they cry out to me, I will not listen to them'" (Jer. 11:10–11).

Bargaining

Many books on prayer describe the negative impact of sin described in the above categories. We need to know these if our prayers are to move forward unhindered. But the simple listing of sins may create another hindrance to prayer. Since our negative actions limit prayer's power, we may be tempted to believe our positive actions are responsible for prayer's effectiveness. Without question "the prayer of a righteous man is powerful and effective" (James 5:16), but is the righteousness of the man the source of prayer's effectiveness? Can we buy God's prayer favors with our goodness?

In the Sermon on the Mount, Jesus teaches his disciples how to pray, and he cautions, "And when you pray, do not keep on babbling like pagans, for they think they will be heard because of their many words" (Matt. 6:7). The word for "babbling" connotes repeating words to gain attention. But what's so wrong with repetition? Christians around the world repeat the words of the Lord's Prayer. It's the way Jesus taught us to pray. Jesus himself repeated this prayer later in his ministry (Luke 11).

The problem is not the repetition but the motive behind it. Jesus says that pagans believe they will be heard "because of their many words." Repeating words is *not* wrong, but the idea that the duration, eloquence, or multiplication of our words will obligate God to act as we wish is a hindrance to prayer.

When we depend on the quantity or quality of our prayer (or fasting or study or sacrifice) to determine its spiritual effectiveness, we imprison God within the limits of our abilities. We shut him within the confines of self-effort whenever we presume we can dredge up words numerous enough or refined enough to make him perform divine feats for our benefit. We constantly need reminders that our best works are filthy rags before God (Isa. 64:6). Our finest eloquence is stammering ignorance before his mind, and our longest recitations barely register in his infinity. God hears our prayers because of his mercy, not because of our mastery of them or of him. He listens to the words that are sincere and seek to honor him, not because our prayers bribe him but because he loves to honor those who depend on him.

Dependence is marked more by regular and fervent petitions for mercy than by attempts to earn favor through our devotion. We pray primarily because we long to be close to the Father, who loves us despite our failings. When we begin to heap up prayers as bargaining chips to barter for God's mercy, we actually deny his mercy—implying he simply needs to be bought by our exertion. However, when we yearn for his presence and speak to him as children drawing near to the Father we love, we honor his nature and can expect his loving response. Thus the heart behind the words determines faithful prayer more than do the words themselves. The words uttered by a loving child and a manipulative one may vary little, but every father knows which to honor. Our heavenly Father knows too.

A couple we know took a child from the streets into their home. The child of an absent father and a crack-addicted mother, his every action was calculated to gain some advantage over others. A smile was intended either to get attention or to make you drop your guard. A hug was either a way to get a favor or check the size of your wallet. Sadly, not only were his words and actions designed to manipulate, he presumed the same was true of everyone else. He began to change only after an argument ended in a way that his street rules did not explain.

Despite the boy's loud and angry objections, his new parents imposed rules for his obedience. His inability to get his own way made the boy so mad that he began to cry. He left the room and crawled under his bed in anger and embarrassment. His new father soon joined him there. The father explained that in a family people should not walk away from each other just because they are mad, but that if someone does, he is still loved and part of the family. Then, in the darkness under the bed, the boy really hugged his father for the first time. There was no request to change the rules and no effort to barter for some advantage. The hug was just a hug, an expression of love for being accepted just as he was and where he was.

The boy's under-the-bed hug was no different physically from the hundreds of manipulative embraces he had previously given, but it was a vastly different hug because of the change in his heart. So our prayers, though in expression or wording not unlike the prayers of those who are trying to manipulate God, are on another level because of the love that is in our heart. God can distinguish between prayer made frequently and fervently because we desire to be near him and prayer made intense and often because we desire to use him. He is blessed by prayers that are filled with the assurance of his love and is grieved by those that are mere barter for his affection.

Power Promoters

The mark of those who love God is holiness (John 14:15; 1 John 5:3), and holy people can expect him to hear and answer their prayers. "For the eyes of the Lord are on the righteous and his ears are attentive to their prayer, but the face of the Lord is against those who do evil" (1 Peter 3:12). Since God responds to those who seek his ways, we participate in the advancement of God's kingdom when our prayers honor him. Humility and devotion characterize such prayers.

Humility

God does not bless the prayers of the righteous because our goodness warrants or purchases his blessing. Again, we should remember when we have done all that we should do, we are still "unworthy servants" in comparison to God's holiness (Luke 17:10). If God's blessing were dependent on our prayers' adequacy—because they were pure enough, long enough, frequent enough, or fervent enough—then we could expect no blessing. Even if we repented of the inadequacy of our prayer, our repentance could not be complete enough to merit God's kindness.

God does not bless our prayers because they have achieved a sufficient level of perfection to trigger his response. Mercifully Scripture portrays God as blessing those who acknowledge their insufficiency. In Christ's parable of the Pharisee and the tax collector, only the man who acknowledges his unworthiness receives God's mercy (Luke 18:9–14). When a grieving father brings his demon-possessed child to Jesus, the Savior promises healing "for him who believes." The father replies, "I do believe; help me overcome my unbelief!" (Mark 9:24). Then Jesus heals the boy.

Those who confess their need of Christ receive the blessing that Jesus promises to the holy. This message is vital for those of us who fall into the first category rather than the latter. Since we cannot by our best efforts meet the standards of God's holiness, we need to approach God humbly, confessing our need of his mercy and grace, rather than trying to barter for his blessing with our goodness. For sinners like us, humility is the path to God's blessing. This humility is not something we manufacture but something we gain as we confess to God that nothing in us deserves his grace, not our conduct, not our service, not our prayers—not even our humility. Biblical humility says, "Father, I appeal to you in Jesus' name. For his sake and because of his righteousness in my place, hear my prayer."

Devotion

Since our works cannot control a holy God's blessing, there are no magic tricks in the spiritual life. Having the right formula for the words we say or the right regimen for when we say them will not guarantee God's response. Yet there are helpful habits that focus our prayers and aid us in maintaining biblical priorities. Jesus teaches his disciples the Lord's Prayer so they will have a pattern to guide their prayers. The Bible tells us also that through the ages devoted believers have prayed numerous times through the day, during times of worship, at meals, and on special occasions. Prayers vary in length. Believers pray in various postures—kneeling, standing, sitting, prostrate, lying in bed (see 1 Chron. 17:16; 2 Chron. 6:12–13; Ps. 63:6). All of these examples inform, but we should not make any as a touchstone of faithfulness.

The Bible gives us prayer examples to help us develop helpful habits, but refining the attitude of the heart is Scripture's goal. What begins as a mechanical pattern of prayer becomes a habit and then a natural part of our lives. And in this reflexive state of prayer—where prayer is as instinctive as breathing—our habits are not rules or rituals intended to satisfy the demands of God but rather the familiar doorways to a constant and spontaneous outpouring of the heart. These doors lead to devotional lives of unceasing prayer—constrained not by any legal compulsion but by love for the God who is always listening (1 Thess. 5:16–18).

In the ordinary progress of the Christian life, we typically learn to pray in the pattern of the Lord's Prayer, the A-C-T-S acrostic (adoration, confession, thanksgiving, supplication), or the PPP method (praise, petition, and praise). We study the prayers of faithful men and women through the ages to help mature our prayers.[3] Since we want to pray with the mind of Christ, it's also helpful to pray using the words of Scripture inspired by his Spirit.[4] We can read a passage slowly and pray about the concerns or praises the text brings to mind. We can also orient our prayers to God's priorities by inserting our names and concerns in the promises of Scripture.

Christians pray more spontaneously when our regular habits make prayer natural rather than unusual. Prayer before meals, during daily devotions, and at bedtime make prayer a familiar part of life. The Scriptures record such habits, and these habits can accustom entire families to speaking to God (Ps. 55:17; Dan. 6:10–12; Luke 24:30). Regular patterns of family prayer help children grow up naturally praying to God—and automatically expecting him to listen.

I once found my wife crying quietly at our back door. I asked what was wrong. "Nothing," she whispered, and then with a smile she pointed toward the backyard. There our two preschool sons had taken their peanut butter and jelly sandwiches for an impromptu picnic. But before they ate, they were bowing their heads and praying. Prayer was as natural to them as eating, and their God was as familiar to them as food. We cherished the blessing and still treasure the memory that reminds us how real and present God is to those who regularly draw near to him.

For the sake of our testimony to others and to honor God, believers also include prayer in our corporate worship, on special occasions, and whenever we feel moved to seek, thank, or praise God. No matter the prayer pattern we adopt, however, we should remember there are many patterns of prayer in Scripture, including the simple cry for help in time of distress.

We discern whether our patterns of prayer are accomplishing God's purposes by asking ourselves *why* we are praying so habitually. Honestly evaluating whether our habits are leading to natural expressions of praise and petition will help us enjoy entering and returning to the presence of God. Are our prayers only spiritual coins being shoved into the slot machine in the sky—methodically, ritualistically, and mechanically—with the hope of a divine payout? Or are our habits truly doors through which we regularly enter our Father's care and humble ourselves before his wisdom while delighting in doing his will?

Perhaps the best measure of the impact of our habitual prayers is the frequency of impromptu prayer in our lives. When our habits are producing biblical fruit, we are constantly talking to God and delighting that we can. We shoot arrow prayers to heaven throughout the day, whispering a word of thanks for the parking space, seeking a word of wisdom for a conversation, and asking for a safe trip home from school. We constantly talk to God as a dear Friend. We also long more and more for the scheduled times of prayer in our private devotion and corporate worship that refresh our sense of his presence and care.

Backwards into the Future

When life becomes immersed in prayer, increasingly we understand that we take no step without God's aid, and we take every step forward with his blessing. We rejoice that nothing enters a life of prayer except that which God intends for the good of the believer and the glory of our Savior. More and more we perceive that the world moves forward under the impulse of our God as he lovingly answers prayer. Thus we pray without ceasing, knowing our future is shaped by the prayers of those who appeal to the Father by the Spirit in the name of the Son. Jesus' name naturally becomes the beginning and end of our prayer because his glory is the beginning and end of all things—and we know all these things are being worked together for our good.

Praying in Jesus' name is not merely the postscript to a good prayer; it is the prelude to God's providing the best of all things for his loved ones. Putting the name of Jesus first when we pray is not really praying backwards. Such prayer is actually putting first the purposes of the One whose glory and delight it is to give us the best of earth and heaven forever. By praying backwards, we always move forward with the assurance God will use whatever life brings for the Savior's glory and our good. He can do no less than provide his best for those who offer prayer in Jesus' name. Such prayer is our great privilege, power, and peace.

Several years ago we took our children on a canoe trip. My wife, Kathy, sat in the front of the canoe holding our three-year-old daughter. I steered in back while my two sons paddled from the middle. After a stretch of calm water, the currents began to quicken. We were not scared until the canoe in front of us suddenly disappeared. It simply dropped from sight on an open stretch of water. At first, we did not understand. Then as the water began to race past us and we heard the sound of crashing water, we realized the danger ahead—a waterfall!

The currents rushed us toward the drop, and our three-year-old began to cry. But as we approached the drop, we could see that safety lay in a narrow channel that skirted the edge of the waterfall and led through rapids to the lower stream. I shouted, "Paddle, boys, paddle." My wife screamed, "And pray."

We barely made the channel, plunged down the rapids, and made it into the lower stream drenched but upright. Howling with laughter and excitement, the boys yelled, "We made it!" Kathy shouted to the sky, "Thank you, Lord!" We had paddled hard, but we knew, as we watched canoe after canoe behind us tumble down the falls (which were really only about five feet high), that the Lord had carried us through.

Somehow that episode has become a metaphor of life for our family. Kathy has written of it in her stories[5] and both of us refer to it often when we address church groups. We encourage others to paddle hard through the challenges the Lord places before them, but at the same time we remind everyone and ourselves to pray to the One who carries us forward according to his perfect plan. The currents of life will sweep everyone forward, but there is peace in the knowledge that as we entrust ourselves to God and seek the glory of his Son, he grants us the power to paddle where the streams are most blessed.

Key Thought: God shapes our world through the prayers of those who appeal to the Father by the Spirit in the name of the Son. Jesus' name is the beginning and end of our prayer because his glory is the beginning and end of all things—and all these things are being worked together for our good. Praying in Jesus' name is not merely the postscript to a good prayer; it is the prelude to God's providing the best of all things for his loved ones.

Praying Christ's Kingdom Forward

Great God of All Things Seen and Unseen,
I come to you today in the mighty name of
    Jesus.
Through him
    who brought the universe into being
    and who continues to sustain all things by
        his powerful Word
    and who loved me enough to shed
        his blood for my soul,
I now ask you to extend your sovereign rule
    over my life.

Transform your creation through my prayers
    as they are transported to you
        by the wisdom of the Spirit and
        by the intercession of Jesus.
Transform me
    by your Word and Spirit
    working in my heart.

Make my world new
    by making me new
    for the glory of my Savior.
Move Christ's kingdom forward

by using my prayers
for the reign of my Savior.

Radiate my King's glory
from my humble petitions;
Winnow his good
from my wayward requests;
Immerse my ransomed life
in his richest purposes.
May Christ be with me, Christ within me,
Christ behind me, Christ before me,
Christ beneath me, Christ over me.
I confess my constant need of his eternal grace,
and
I profess his unending supply.

May Jesus Christ be praised
in me and by me,
As I rejoice now and forever in Jesus' name.
Amen

Conclusion

In Jesus' Name, Amen

I once had the privilege of caring for a small, aging German lump of sugar named Mae Gabriel. Mae was in her late eighties. She still knew much of her German Bible and spent the day humming the hymns of her youth, though she could barely hear.

Mae lived alone in a two-room house on her son-in-law's farm. Her prized possessions were a velvet leaf plant that had practically taken over her kitchen, dusty photos of her family on a bedroom bureau, and a skunk that wandered out of the woods at dusk to eat scraps she put out on a cracked dinner plate. In many ways you could consider Mae pitiable—even pathetic. But Mae Gabriel was a saint. She taught me as much about prayer as anyone I have ever known.

During one of my visits, Mae told me of the death of her husband. Frank had died twenty years earlier, but when she spoke of him, her eyes still brimmed with tears. She told me about the day the doctors said Frank had only a short time left. On that day Mae said she prayed over and over that God would heal Frank. "I didn't want to be alone," she said with a smile.

Then she told me how she prayed.

"First, I prayed that God's will would be done," she said with a determined nod of her head. "Then I prayed again and again that the Lord would heal my husband. But I also prayed that if he needed to take Frank, my God would give me the strength to bear it."

Then in the midst of Mae's tears, a beautiful smile lit up her whole face as though her heart were shining through. She simply said, "And he did. God gave me the strength to bear it."

Mae prayed backwards. She prayed first for the priorities of her God—that his will would be done. Then she prayed her desires. She boldly and persistently petitioned for her husband. Again and again this little woman knocked against the door of heaven without hesitation or shame. She listed her specific wants, but she also voiced the deeper desire for God to do his will. She did not doubt or fear the hand of the heavenly Father, who had given his own Son to be her eternal Savior.

By praying in this holy, humble, and trusting way, Mae knew that whatever God chose to do would be best, not only for this world but also for eternity. Mae's knowledge of God's nature shaped her prayer, sustained her faith, and brought her strength for her time of sorrow. She simply prayed as Jesus taught, and she gained the peace he promised.

Jesus taught us never to voice a prayer we could not pray backwards. We utter every petition with a heart of praise, seeking first the honor of our Savior. Praying in Jesus' name is ultimately no sacrifice because he chooses to glorify himself by providing the best of his kingdom for his people. When the greatest desire of our heart is his glory, the greatest joy of his heart is our blessing.

We pray in Jesus' name because we have the blessed assurance that the Father will do for the sake of his Son all that is best for him and those he loves. With this confidence, we have the privilege, joy, and peace to pray to him again and again, "Thy will be done. In Jesus' name, amen."

Discussion Questions

Introduction: Praying for Change

1. How would your prayer priorities change if you began where you normally end?
2. How do we limit God by our wisdom if we treat prayer like a heavenly wishing well?
3. If God does not promise to relieve all suffering as a consequence of our prayer, why should we pray?
4. How should praying in Jesus' name sensitize us to his priorities?
5. How should Jesus' priorities change our prayers?

Chapter 1: Praying in Jesus' Name

1. How does Jesus show that he is patient about our need to grow in understanding prayer?
2. What is wrong with treating God like a celestial vending machine into which we place faith nickels to get whatever we want through prayer?

3. What is the most important reason for us to pray in Jesus' name?
4. Why do we need to use Jesus' name when we approach God?
5. How does the Holy Spirit respond to our use of Jesus' name in prayer? Why?
6. What is the ultimate purpose of praying in Jesus' name?
7. How do childish prayers contrast with mature prayers truly offered in Jesus' name?

Chapter 2: Praying in Jesus' Way

1. How does the first petition of the Lord's Prayer, "Father, hallowed be your name," teach us to pray for God's purposes as our first priority?
2. How does the second petition of the Lord's Prayer, "Your kingdom come," teach us to pray for God's purposes as our first priority?
3. How does the third petition of the Lord's Prayer, "Give us today our daily bread," teach us to pray for God's purposes as our first priority?
4. How does the fourth petition of the Lord's Prayer, "Forgive us our debts, as we also have forgiven our debtors," teach us to pray for God's purposes as our first priority?
5. How does the fifth petition of the Lord's Prayer, "Lead us not into temptation," teach us to pray for God's purposes as our first priority?
6. Does Jesus urge us to pray this last petition with the expectation that God will tempt us if we don't?
7. What does it mean for you to pray, "Lord, not my will but your will be done"?

Chapter 3: Praying without Doubting

1. Can you pray without doubting that God will provide precisely what you want?
2. Can you pray without doubting that God is able to provide precisely what you want or what he knows is better?
3. How is the object of faith misplaced when we pray that God will provide what *we* think is most desirable?
4. Is it always an "escape hatch" prayer or "hedging" our faith to pray, "Yet, Lord, not my will but your will be done"? Why or why not?
5. How do Jesus and the apostles qualify God's promise to give "whatever you want in prayer"? In what context does this promise always reside?
6. Of what benefit is it to trust in God's sovereignty when we pray?
7. Does God always answer our prayers for healing? What are God's possible ways of answering such prayers according to his sovereign and eternal purposes?
8. Why is it better to ask God to heal *according* to his will than to heal *if* it is his will?

Chapter 4: Praying in the Spirit

1. Why should we ask God to respond to our prayers if he already knows our needs?
2. How does the Holy Spirit provide the fervor that may be lacking in our prayers?
3. How does the Holy Spirit provide the wisdom that may be lacking in our prayers?
4. How does the Holy Spirit provide the power that may be lacking in our prayers?

5. If we are not primarily concerned for the Lord's purposes, should we expect God to answer our prayers? What are evidences in Scripture that support your answer?
6. How can the Holy Spirit not only turn our prayers to Jesus' priorities but also actually make these priorities our desires?
7. How does the desire for Christ's purposes provide us the power to fulfill them?
8. Why is the privilege of praying in the Holy Spirit the greatest power and privilege that God can grant to a believer?

Chapter 5: Praying Boldly

1. How does praying in Jesus' name grant us a new and privileged identity as we pray?
2. Why should we be willing to "impose" on our heavenly Father when we pray in Jesus' name?
3. Why should we be willing to petition our heavenly Father for matters both large and small when we pray in Jesus' name?
4. How should the privileges of praying in Jesus' name affect the frequency and consistency of our prayers?
5. How should the privileges of praying in Jesus' name affect the formality or familiarity of our prayers?
6. How should the privileges of praying in Jesus' name affect our willingness to pray for miracles?
7. How boldly should we pray? Why?

Chapter 6: Praying Expectantly

1. Should we pray with the expectation that God will answer specific prayers?
2. How is specific prayer an act of worship?

3. How is submissive prayer an act of worship?
4. How do specific and submissive prayers avoid unhealthy patterns that lead to generic and infrequent requests?
5. What evidence does Scripture offer that God encourages specific prayer but does not expect our earthly desires to determine his eternal will?
6. How is prayer the Christian's artillery in God's war for the world?
7. How does corporate prayer aid our prayers and God's purposes?
8. How do we complete and correct one another in corporate prayer so that Christ's voice comes from his church body?

Chapter 7: Praying Persistently

1. Is it wrong to pray again and again for the same thing? What guidance does the Bible offer regarding persistent prayer?
2. What are reasons that we do not persist in prayer?
3. What are some reasons that God may desire persistent prayer?
4. Is it wrong to voice frustration and disappointment in prayer? What examples does the Bible offer of such prayers?
5. What good can it do to offer our frustrations to God in prayer? What good would it do to hide our frustrations from God?
6. What may God be accomplishing through persistent prayer that is better than what we originally pray? How does persistence refine our prayers?
7. How does God create Christlikeness by persistent prayer? How does persistence refine us?

8. What would be the consequences if we could snap our fingers and get God to perform whatever we wanted immediately?

Chapter 8: Praying in God's Will

1. What questions come to your mind when you are told that God will answer whatever you ask that is according to his will?
2. How do you determine if a prayer is within the fence of righteousness? What should we trust more than personal feelings or priorities to help us make this determination?
3. Why is it more important to obey God's will in prayer than to try to predict his will?
4. What can we pray with the absolute assurance that it will match God's will?
5. What are problems with assigning moral values to legitimate options that God provides? Are some apples in a fruit basket more righteous than others? How does your answer affect how you should respond to the blessings of multiple options?
6. What are the problems with asking for God to provide external or miraculous "signs" to direct our decisions?
7. How does trusting that God is our Good Shepherd enable us to pray correctly and consistently?
8. How does trusting that God is our Good Shepherd enable us to find peace on the path he designs even when we do not know all that is ahead?

Chapter 9: Praying in God's Wisdom

1. How should biblical principles be weighed when determining if our desires or decisions are prudent? Does

Christian prudence ever dispense with the issues of right and wrong?

2. How do the principles of biblical love affect our understanding of whether our prayers are prudent?

3. How do the principles of biblical legitimacy affect our understanding of whether our prayers are prudent?

4. How do the principles of biblical responsibility affect our understanding of whether our prayers are prudent?

5. What role do subjective or internal "feelings" have in helping us determine if our prayers are prudent? How does the Holy Spirit use these feelings to help guide us?

6. Should such internal "feelings" ever be weighed more heavily than biblical instructions or principles? How do we test whether what we are feeling is the witness of the Holy Spirit in our hearts?

7. What role do circumstances play in helping us determine if our prayers are prudent?

8. If our prayers are within the fences of Christian righteousness and prudence, do we need to fear that we are ever outside of God's will?

Chapter 10: Praying Forward

1. Why is a conversation with God an inadequate description of prayer? What wrong expectations might the conversation metaphor create?

2. How do the words that we speak to God both become his words and shape the world before us in which he is working?

3. How do the words we speak to God change the realities we see and enable us to perceive his greater realities?

4. How does the assurance that God really listens to our prayers change us and our world?

5. How does sin hinder our prayers?

6. How does using prayer to bargain for divine favors actually damage our prayers?
7. What role does humility have in our prayers? Why?
8. How does noting the frequency and spontaneity of our prayers help diagnose the true motivation behind our prayers?
9. Does it encourage you to know that God can do no less than provide his best for those who pray in Jesus' name? How does this encourage you?

Notes

Chapter 2 Praying in Jesus' Way

1. From personal correspondence of Bill Kuh, November 24, 2003. The letter is alleged to have been found on the body of an unknown soldier after the Battle of Gettysburg. The letter appears in many sources. One of the best is the history teachers' web page, "Civil War Battles and Generals," at http://www.adjutant.com/other/confederate_prayer.htm.

2. "Let's Roll," *World* (September/October 2002): 28.

Chapter 3 Praying without Doubting

1. PreachingNow@preaching.com, vol. 3, no. 17 (May 3, 2004).

2. From a transcription of an address that Dr. James Montgomery Boice gave to the congregation of Tenth Presbyterian Church in Philadelphia, May 7, 2000, available at http://www.tenth.org/boiceupdate.html.

Chapter 4 Praying in the Spirit

1. C. S. Lewis, *The Magician's Nephew* (1955; repr., New York: HarperCollins, 1994), 163.

2. Thomas Chalmers, *Sermons and Discourses*, vol. 2 (New York: Carter, 1846), 271.

3. Sinclair Ferguson, *The Holy Spirit* (Downers Grove, IL: InterVarsity, 1996), 122.

4. See Sinclair Ferguson, "The Reformed View," in *Christian Spirituality: Five Views of Sanctification* (Downers Grove, IL: InterVarsity, 1988), 69, 71.

Chapter 5 Praying Boldly

1. Joe Wheeler, "Evensong," in *Family News from Dr. James Dobson* (December 2002): 2.

2. Helmut Thielicke, *Encounter with Spurgeon* (Philadelphia: Fortress, 1963), 1.

3. Origen, *Treatise on Prayer, De Oratione*, XXXIII, 1.

Chapter 6 Praying Expectantly

1. Adapted from John Houghton, *The Search for God* (Oxford: Lion, 1995), 163–64.

2. These citations from chapter 10 of A. T. Pierson, *George Mueller of Bristol*, available at http://www.whatsaiththescripture.com/Voice/George.Mueller.of.Bristol/George.Mueller.of.Bristol.html.

3. Rick Gray, prayer letter from Uganda, December 1991.

4. Os Guinness, *The Call* (Dallas: Word, 1998), 183–85.

5. Thomas Manton, *Collected Works: James*, 461.

6. Leaflets describing these events were still available at the door of the church at least as late as 1998.

Chapter 7 Praying Persistently

1. Basil Miller, *George Muller: Man of Faith and Miracles* (Minneapolis: Bethany, 1972), 146.

2. David J. Michell, "After the Gold," *Heart Values*, available at www.heartvalues.com/eric_Liddell_after_the_gold.html (2004), 4.

3. Ibid., 5.

4. Ibid.

5. "Eric Liddell, More Than an Olympic Champion," *Christian History Institute* 161, available at www.gospelcom.net/chi/GLIMPSEF/glmps161.shtml (2004), 1.

6. As quoted by Tom Schwanda in "Be Still and Know How to Pray," *Reformed Bible College News* 36, no. 1 (September/October 2000): 8.

7. John Calvin, *Institutes*, III, xx, 3.

Chapter 8 Praying in God's Will

1. Email to Susan Breeding, edited and forwarded by her husband, Bruce (September 25, 2003). Used with permission.

2. Email forwarded by Rev. Bob Flayhart on July 24, 2002, and used with permission of Jason and Susie Tucker.

Chapter 9 Praying in God's Wisdom

1. Personal conversation with Eric Alexander, St. Louis, April 17, 2002.

Chapter 10 Praying Forward

1. Quoted in J. Michael Bennett, *Four Powers of Communication: Skills for Effective Learning* (New York: McGraw-Hill, 1991), 51.

2. *St. Louis Post-Dispatch* (May 3, 2001).

3. For example, see Arthur Bennett, *The Valley of Vision: A Collection of Puritan Prayers* (1975; repr., Carlisle, PA: Banner of Truth, 2002); Richard Foster and James Bryan Smith, *Devotional Classics: Selected Readings for Individuals and Groups* (1990; repr., San Francisco: HarperCollins, 1993); or Leonard Ravenhill, *A Treasury of Prayer:*

The Best of E. M. Bounds (1961; repr., Minneapolis: Bethany, 1981). Note that phrases and ideas from a number of ancient prayers are worked into the prayer at the end of this chapter.

4. See Kenneth Boa's excellent *Face to Face: Praying the Scriptures for Intimate Worship* (Grand Rapids: Zondervan, 1997).

5. Kathy Chapell, *Devotions for Ministry Wives*, ed. Barbara Hughes (Grand Rapids: Zondervan, 2002), 118–19.

Bryan Chapell is the president of Covenant Theological Seminary in St. Louis. Raised in Memphis, Tennessee, Dr. Chapell pastored for ten years before joining the faculty of Covenant Seminary.

Dr. Chapell speaks at churches, colleges, and seminaries throughout the country and abroad. He is also an accomplished author, church leader, and father of four. He and his wife, Kathleen, have devoted their lives to helping others rejoice in the power and peace of the gospel of grace in Christ Jesus.

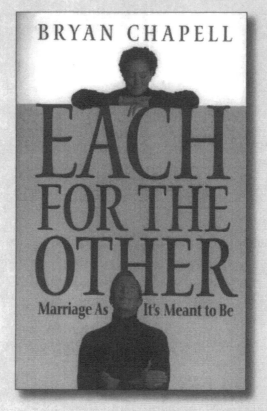

Made in the USA
San Bernardino, CA
07 October 2013